STILL LOADING

BECAUSE GROWTH DOESN'T COME WITH A FINAL VERSION...

AUTHOR

AMAN KHATRI

Latika Teotia Publishing House

@latikateotia.com

For Parth

Preface

A Friendly Disclaimer Before You Proceed

If you've picked up this book hoping for a life-altering corporate success guide, put it back before it's too late. What you'll find here are life lessons that took their sweet time to show up, wisdom still a work in progress, and a few bumps along the way that somehow turned into stories. So, lower your expectations, grab a cup of coffee, and enjoy the ride.

This isn't the story of a superhero, a startup genius, or the next TED Talk sensation. "This is my story, Aman..." -a very average boy who once thought climbing trees was a viable career option and genuinely believed his mother's cooking could solve world peace.

Along the way, I learned the hard way that life has a sense of humor funnier than mine. Somewhere between the carefree days of childhood games and the meticulous chaos of corporate life -where Excel sheets are worshipped and "synergy" is a buzzword -I figured out that the real syllabus was never in my school bag. And the tests? They never stopped.

So, whether you're a 20-something rookie still trying to crack the code of office small talk, or a seasoned professional wondering when your social life got outsourced to your calendar app -I hope this book gives you a moment (or two) to grin at the mess we call growing up.

And if nothing else, let this book remind you:

Growing up is mandatory.

Growing old is inevitable.

But growing dull? That's entirely optional.

Welcome aboard. Buckle up. Life, as I've learned, rarely follows the GPS.

– Aman

Contents

Preface   *vii*

Chapter 1   "MBA: Mission Bangalore Again"   1

Chapter 2   Confessions of a Couch Commando   7

Chapter 3   No Lanyard, Just LinkedIn   17

Chapter 4   Silver Bells and First Hellos   23

Chapter 5   "Homes in Transit"   29

Chapter 6   "Benchmates & Break Times"   41

Chapter 7   The MBA Remix: UK Edition   79

Chapter 8   "Monday to Monday:
                    The Corporate Loop"   105

Chapter 9   "The Corporate Balancing Act"   113

Epilogue   *Suit Up, Life's Still Loading!!!*   *121*

About the Author   *127*

Chapter 1

"MBA: Mission Bangalore Again"

The drive to the airport was a mix of emotions- Papa, as usual, serious and focused. Mummy, as expected, non-stop with her dos and don'ts.

Papa was at the wheel, hands at ten and two, posture straight, gaze fixed ahead. Years of Army discipline meant he drove with quiet precision-no abrupt moves, no unnecessary honking, just a steady, controlled pace as if the road itself had rules only he truly respected.

Mummy sat in the back, instructions flowing non-stop- 'Call every day. And eat healthy. No junk food, okay? Don't tell me later that you're surviving on chips and instant noodles.

I nodded, pretending to check my phone but mostly staring out at the familiar roads of Chandigarh, trying to ignore the weight of leaving.

Chandigarh does that to you. It isn't just a city-it's comfort, predictability, order. Wide roads, neatly numbered sectors, and those identical roundabouts where you always feel like you've taken the wrong turn but somehow end up exactly where you need to be. It's like an old favorite song; you know every beat, every pause, and no matter how many new ones you hear, this is the one that always feels like home.

Of course, growing up in an Army family, I had seen my fair share of cities. Transfers, new houses, new schools, new friends, new routines- it was just how life worked. But there was a difference between moving cities with your family and moving alone. At 19, I had the confidence of someone who thought that he had seen it all. Turns out, I hadn't.

Mummy wasn't done. "And listen, whatever happens, any problem, call Devekar Uncle. He's right there in Bangalore. At least visit him once in a while, okay?"

I nodded again. It was easier than arguing.

Papa finally spoke, his voice steady, like always. "You'll manage." Classic Army parenting- minimum words, maximum expectations.

The airport was in sight now. One-way ticket. New city. No cantonment safety net.

Papa helped unload my bag, then said, "Call when you land."

Mummy pulled me into a quick hug. "And listen, just be yourself."

I smirked. "Of course, Mummy. Who else would I be?"

She sighed. "That's what I'm afraid of."

I laughed, picked up my bag, and walked toward the departure gate.

It was time.

I touched Papa and Mummy's feet- because that's what we do. No matter how old you are, in Indian families, a journey isn't official until you've bent down for blessings, whether you're going to war or just changing cities.

Mummy, of course, wasn't satisfied with just that. She again pulled me into a hug, like I was 11 again, leaving for Military School. That time, I barely lasted a handful of days before returning- thanks to certain medical issues (which you'll soon hear about). Turns out, my body had strong opinions about the food and flavors of Bangalore.

And now, here I was, heading back. As if Bangalore had been sitting there all these years, tapping its foot impatiently, waiting for my grand return. "Come back, Aman. Unfinished business remains!"

Or maybe I was just a slow learner. Either way, Bangalore and I had a score to settle.

Mummy let out a deep sigh and reached up to fix my hair, like she always did before any big moment in my life. It was her signature move- one final attempt at setting my life in order, one stray strand at a time. I'd never understood her logic, but then again, logic and mothers don't always go hand in hand.

Honestly, it amuses me. I'm sure many of you have been through this- mothers don't see their child for his actual age; they pick whichever version of you suits their mood. Today, apparently I was still a schoolboy.

And it doesn't matter where you are- club, boardroom, formal function, or in a market- for mothers, it's always home when it comes to their kids. No filters, no hesitation. If you need a scolding, you'll get it in front of an audience. If they feel affectionate, they'll ruffle your hair like you're five- even if your friends are watching. And if you politely tell them, "Please don't do this," be prepared for a big sullen face, prolonged sulking, and an inevitable lecture. Obviously, your heart will melt, and you'll start seeing it as her way of loving you unconditionally- or as you loving her unconditionally. Either way, you don't stand a chance.

In fact, sometimes I think we're the real adults in this equation. Mothers? They're the truly carefree, unfiltered souls. And maybe that's what makes them so special.

Anyway, I hugged her back, holding on for a moment longer than usual. Then, with a deep breath, I turned to leave-only to catch one last glimpse of her tearful eyes.

Fathers, on the other hand, are different. Their version of an emotional farewell is a firm nod, a pat on the back, and a gruff "Take care." But that's just their way of saying everything they won't put into words.

As the flight took off, I stared out of the window, watching Chandigarh shrink beneath me. The last time I was on a plane to Bangalore, I was 11, sitting next to Papa, all set for Military School. That adventure had lasted about as long as a North Indian's patience in a slow-moving queue. My stomach, forever loyal to parathas and butter, had staged a full-scale rebellion against the flavors of Bangalore. Dosas, sambhar, coconut chutney- it was as if my digestive system had taken a solemn oath never to entertain such southern experiments. A few months in, I was back home, looking like I had barely survived a war, while Mummy tried very hard not to say, "I told you so."

And yet, here I was again. Maybe, Bangalore had some karmic grip on me. Maybe, in a past life, I had offended a dosa vendor by calling it 'dosa' instead of 'dōse,' and now, fate was dragging me back for linguistic and culinary atonement.

Or maybe Bangalore had simply decided, "Enough of your tantrums, Aman. Time to toughen up and embrace the dōse life."

They say MBA is the place where you find yourself. I wasn't entirely sure what that meant-because if anything, MBA reminded me just how many versions of myself I'd already lived.

From a tree-climbing army brat to a stitched-up indoor strategist, from console warrior to campus candidate in business-casual-if *self-reinvention* were a sport, I'd already be an Olympian.

And yet, here I was, expected to *"find myself"*-as if that one final version was just hiding behind a PowerPoint deck or waiting at the end of a group discussion.

Most guys in my batch talked about their childhood cricket tournaments or football rivalries like they were reliving scenes from Chak De! India. Me? I had more experience scoring goals on a PlayStation controller than on an actual field. My best athletic feats were limited to mastering Mortal Kombat combos and saving the world with the SWAT Kats, one joystick flick at a time.

Not that I didn't love the outdoors. I did. I truly did.

Until I was six.

Chapter 2

Confessions of a Couch Commando

That was the year everything changed.

One day, I was a tiny, over-enthusiastic dynamite-climbing trees like Tarzan's understudy, jumping off staircases like I was auditioning for *SWAT Kats*, and stealthily navigating the backyard like a six-year-old Army commando on a top secret mission (call sign: "Ninja Mango"). My camouflage? Mud-stained half-pants and a scraped knee. My weapon? A branch I found under the guava tree. My enemy? Imaginary terrorists hiding behind Mummy's flower pots.

And then, boom. Life flipped.

Literally.

It started like one of those perfect family days, the kind you wish came with a "repeat" button.

Destination: Indore.

Mood: Festive.

Battery level: 100%.

After a full day of running around like a sugar-powered tornado, we landed at Hotel Mashaal for dinner, still riding the high of the Dussehra holidays .

And that's when I saw it.

The swing.

Majestic. Mysterious. Slightly off-balance. But to my six-year-old eyes, it looked like the gateway to greatness. I charged toward it like Popeye on a spinach high-pumped, fearless, and blissfully unaware of the disaster waiting to unfold.

Seconds later, I was airborne.

Legs up, heart racing, hair doing its own dance.

I was swinging like I'd just been recruited by the Swat Kats, living my best daredevil dream. And then-THUD.

A loose iron rod decided to go rogue and crash into my stomach like Bluto ambushing Popeye-minus the spinach.

No blood. No visible injury.

But the pain? Oh boy.

The scream I let out deserved a Zee Horror Show zoom-in-complete with thunderclap, lightning strike, and a dramatic violin screech.

My inner monologue went full soap opera:

"Yeh kya ho gaya?!"

I didn't know what had just happened, but I knew one thing for sure-

This wasn't part of the cartoon.

We rushed to the Military Hospital in Mhow, where the doctor casually prescribed Brufen, as if I'd stubbed my toe during P.T. Yep, Brufen. As if I had twisted an ankle in P.T. class. I think even my appendix raised an eyebrow. My intestines, meanwhile, were planning a full-blown revolt.

Mummy's instinct went into Zee TV "maa-mode". Mummy tried turmeric milk and every desi trick in the book to comfort me. But when I vomited that golden milk like I'd been possessed by some turmeric demon, , mummy's sixth sense kicked in-the same one that detects lies, sugar binges, and untied shoelaces. She didn't sleep that night. Sat by my side like a soldier in a trench, telling me stories while silently praying to every deity on speed dial.

Then came the morning of Navmi. While most homes were busy preparing prasad, we were preparing for the worst. My pain had mysteriously spread to my underarms-yep, turns out abdominal trauma doesn't care much for anatomy textbooks. Instead of just hurting where it was supposed to (hello, stomach?), the pain decided to take a detour and show up in my armpits like it had booked a connecting flight.

Apparently, underarm pain can be referred pain from the abdomen. (I only found that out once Google entered our lives-because adult me Googles everything. At six, I was just wondering if my arm had developed a personality.)

Anyway, panic hit fast. I was rushed to a private clinic, where the ultrasound revealed the real horror show: internal bleeding. Next stop-Choithram Hospital, Indore.

Now here's where things escalated faster than a Doordarshan soap opera climax.

The team of doctors, led by the heroic surgeon Dr. Amitabh Goel, finally cracked the code. My pancreas had ruptured-yes, the thing that sounds like it belongs in a science quiz. My large intestine had four tears. My small intestine was swimming in blood. Stitching the pancreas, they said, was like trying to sew wet tissue paper-delicate, slippery, and practically defying all laws of surgery.

Only Dr. Amitabh Goel could pull off this next-to-impossible, miraculous task-especially on a tiny six-year-old whose organs had just declared independence.

By the time they were done, I had 8 stitches holding my insides together and 21 on the outside, keeping me from falling apart like a badly wrapped birthday present. That's 29 stitches total-29 reasons to call me what I officially became: the stitched-up ex-commando.

The official report didn't say "enemy fire," but come on-those battle scars were legit. Internal injuries might not look dramatic on the outside, but try telling that to a six-year-old who suddenly can't sit upright, can't eat solid food, and definitely can't jump off sofas yelling, "Shaktimaan!"

I may not have taken a bullet, but inside my belly, it was nothing short of Kargil. A full-blown war zone. And spoiler alert: I wasn't winning that round.

And just like that, my outdoor license was revoked.

Post-surgery, the doctors gave their verdict: "No outdoor sports for three years."

Three. Years !!! For a kid who thought Surf Excel ads were documentaries of his life ("Daag ache hain!"), this was soul-crushing. No football. No running. No climbing trees or jumping staircases. Basically, no acting like me. To six-year-old me, it sounded like a life sentence.

What followed was a forced transformation: from a backyard commando to an indoor strategist. From chasing frogs in the monsoon to commanding peasants in Age of Empires. My physical adventures were replaced by The Jungle Book, SWAT Kats, and long-drawn stand-offs with the TV remote-my only worthy opponent indoors. I couldn't really fight with my baby sister, Apoorva-she was five years younger and looked at me like I was some kind of intergalactic superhero. In her eyes, I wasn't just her brother-I was a stitched-up Shaktimaan-meets-Superman hybrid. That long scar on my stomach? Not the result of emergency surgery, but clear evidence that I'd survived a top-secret space mission and returned with powers no one else had.

I still remember the day she tried to feed me a plastic paratha from her toy kitchen set and called it "emergency recovery food." She could barely string a sentence together, but somehow, I understood everything. That's the thing about being an elder brother-you learn to translate toddler gibberish into love. She was convinced I needed magical nourishment to fully heal and join the Avengers. I played along, of course-bit into that rock-solid plastic chapati like it was Michelin-starred cuisine. Her face lit up like Diwali.

That's the thing about little sisters. You can't fight them, but they'll fight the world for you.

But while Apoorva was my in-house fan club, the outside world had its own plans.

Every evening, like clockwork, the cantonment playground came alive. From 4 to 7 PM, it was our kingdom-echoing with cricket appeals, bicycle bells, and the occasional war cry from a particularly enthusiastic game of chor-police. But not for me. I had been benched by destiny-and by a swing-but oh, did I make that bench look good.

Soon, word got around that I had survived *surgery*. The moment you say that word to a group of kids, it's like saying "superpowers" to a group of Marvel fans.

One by one, my friends started showing up at home. First out of sympathy. Then out of curiosity. And before I knew it-envy.

I had become the proud owner of a belly scar. A real one. Not one of those playground scrapes or bruises you get falling off a cycle. Mine had *stitches*. It had *depth*. It had *mystery*. I wore it like a medal.

And boy, did I sell it well.

You'd think I was offering guided tours: "Step right in, folks. This line here? That's where the doctor stitched me up. Took nineteen of them. No, no-it didn't hurt. I didn't even cry. I just stared at the ceiling fan and recited the alphabet backwards."

The way I narrated it, you'd think I had fought off a tiger, not a faulty swing. I was practically the Shaktimaan of Sector 17.

Some of them-God bless their gullible souls-even asked if they could get a scar too. One chap seriously proposed falling off the see-saw just right. Another offered to exchange his sprained wrist for my belly "badge."

I could barely contain my laughter. But I also didn't want to break the illusion. After all, I was the conman with a stitched-up tale and an audience ready to trade their innocence for a scar story.

Looking back, I think that was my first real sales pitch.

No PowerPoint. No data sheets. Just one dramatic story, a curious audience, and a scar that became my childhood brand.

Mark Twain would've been proud. Probably asked me to whitewash his fence next.

With the playground temporarily out of reach, I found my new turf-on the couch. Entertainment became my playground. Shakalaka Boom Boom made me believe pencils could change the world. Small Wonder had me dreaming of robot siblings (though Apoorva came close-minus the charging port). And Different Strokes? That show taught me that families didn't need to match-they just needed to matter.

Somewhere between channel-surfing and pretending to be Shaktimaan with a towel cape, I was quietly reimagining what "play" meant. I wasn't on the swings or the cricket pitch anymore-but I was building worlds, one episode at a time.

But it was The Sound of Music that truly changed something inside me. Something about the Von Trapps harmonising in the mountains stirred a note I didn't know I had. I started humming along. Then singing. And one day, Papa surprised me with a tiny Casio keyboard-the kind with demo tunes and two good octaves if you pressed hard enough. That's when I realised I wasn't just passively watching music-I could make it. Somewhere between Do-Re-Mi and my first self-composed jingle for Apoorva's dolls, I discovered a voice I didn't know existed.

Maybe I wasn't just an indoor strategist or a remote warrior after all. Maybe, just maybe, I was also a quiet little artist in disguise-finding rhythm in retreat.

Sure, I was alive. But man, childhood looked very different from a sofa cushion.

Still, in hindsight, maybe that accident didn't just change my lifestyle-it changed my lens. It forced me to find other ways to channel that restless energy. Strategy games, storytelling, mimicking Papa's serious tone during phone calls (very effective when you're pretending to run a toy company). I went from playfield warrior to mental gymnast.

Looking back now, I realize that forced pause rewired my world. I shifted gears-from muscle to mind. I became sharper, more observant, even borderline theatrical (you try growing up on a steady diet of *Home Alone, Richie Rich*, and *The Mask* without picking up some flair for drama).

And maybe… just maybe… that detour shaped the version of me that would one day navigate corporate hallways with a straight face, give serious nods during client meetings, and pretend that quarterly targets are thrilling.

Because when you've survived a rogue swing, ruptured pancreas, and three years without football, you develop a quiet kind of superpower. You become adaptable. Resilient. Ready for curveballs-whether from life or from Excel.

And honestly? This whole MBA-life thing-group discussions, presentations, competitive case study brawls-it's basically *Commando 2.0*. Just with blazers instead of bruises. And slightly better grammar.

Chapter 3

No Lanyard, Just LinkedIn

They say every scar tells a story.

Mine told the tale of a six-year-old who flew too close to the swing-and crash-landed into a life he never saw coming.

One day, I was chasing imaginary terrorists with a stick and my G.I. Joes as backup. The next, I was indoors-playing Monopoly with Mummy, crashing remote-control cars into furniture, setting up G.I. Joe battlefields under the dining table, and pretending Mario Kart was as thrilling as the real world outside.

Life didn't just throw a curveball-it threw an iron rod.

And just like that, my childhood got a new script. One that involved less running, more sitting. Less football, more folding paper planes. Less of *who I was,* and more of *who I had to become.*

Three years! That's practically a lifetime when you're six. It's like asking a fish not to swim or a Punjabi boy not to dance at weddings.

So while other kids were out chasing cricket balls and falling into muddy puddles, I was inside-trying to beat Mario Kart and make peace with "indoor life." It wasn't a choice. It was a compromise stitched into my tiny six-year-old belly, right along with those twenty-nine stitches.

That early switch-from cleats to cushions, fields to consoles-left a mark. I guess that's when the tug between outdoor and indoor really began. One part of me still longed to sprint, jump, scrape knees and get yelled at by Mummy for dirtying my clothes. The other part had grown used to a controlled, safe, air-conditioned existence. A life of remote controls, comic books, and later, Excel sheets.

Maybe that's why the MBA-with its debates, deadlines, and endless presentations-felt strangely familiar. It was structured chaos, fought from behind a laptop screen. A battlefield where posture mattered more than stamina.

And while others bragged about their endurance on treks and marathons, I quietly celebrated my own victories-like not having a panic attack before public speaking, or biting into a samosa guilt-free, because yes, my doctor had finally cleared it. A small win, but when your digestive system has been treated like royalty since age six, even street food feels like rebellion.

I wasn't unfit-I was just... selectively fit. Mentally athletic, if you will.

But somewhere deep inside, that six-year-old boy who once raced the wind hadn't given up. He just adapted. And now, as I sat through campus interviews in my perfectly ironed shirt and practiced smile, I wondered if life was nudging me once again-back into the open.

Back into the unknown.

By the way, have you ever noticed how doctor's kids almost always end up becoming doctors? It's like some sacred family ritual. "Welcome to the clan, beta. Here's your stethoscope, your first copy of Gray's Anatomy, and a lab coat two sizes too big-you'll grow into it, just like the pressure."

Surgeon dads, of course, go all in. Their kids don't get Lego sets-they get toy organs and a plastic scalpel. "This is your appendix model, son. And remember, precision over speed. Even in play."

Forget fairy tales-these kids fall asleep to stories about rare diseases and miraculous recoveries. The only monsters under their beds are misdiagnoses.

Actors are no different. One generation's Bollywood royalty retires with a national award, and the next waltzes onto Koffee with Karan before they've even faced a director, let alone a camera. They say it's not nepotism-it's just "legacy." Right. Legacy wrapped in designer couture and launched with a hashtag campaign.

Their idea of struggle? Shooting in Ladakh… without Wi-Fi.

Acting chops? Optional. Last name? Mandatory.

And emotional depth? Mostly visible when the camera pans in slow motion with background violins.

It's not just showbiz-it's showbirth.

Politicians? Ah, that's hereditary monarchy with elections thrown in for flair. Their kids don't just inherit surnames, they inherit entire constituencies-like it's a family heirloom.

"Beta, yeh Lok Sabha seat tere dadaji ki thi. Sambhal ke rakhna."

Cricketers too! One Test match and suddenly the entire nation is Googling if their son can swing a bat at age four. Before the kid learns cursive, he's already got a profile on Cricbuzz.

Even chefs aren't spared. You'll find little Aarav stirring quinoa on YouTube at age seven, with 50k followers and a brand deal for gluten-free cupcakes.

There's something comforting about sticking to the family lane. Less confusion, fewer wrong turns. The GPS already knows the route-just switch drivers.

Me? I wanted to be in the Army. Surprise, surprise.

After all, I was raised in olive green. My bedtime stories were about valour, strategy, and surviving with stale parathas on a snow-clad post. My childhood heroes weren't cricketers or movie stars-they were the men in uniform I saw at the breakfast table. So naturally, the dream was clear. I was going to be the next in line. Not in politics, not on a film set, not in an operation theatre-but on a parade ground, saluting the tricolour and yelling, "Yes sir!"

And I didn't just dream-I tried.

I cleared the exam, aced the interview, saluted my way through SSB with the confidence of someone who had practiced drill commands in his sleep. And then, the medical board politely held up a red flag, like a strict referee at a school match.

"Abdominal history," they said. "Not fit for duty."

Just like that, my Army dreams were honorably discharged, courtesy of a pancreas that couldn't mind its own business back when I was six.

I wanted to argue, to protest: "But I've been carrying this belly like a responsible citizen for years! I even skipped *golgappas* in Class 10!"

But apparently, that doesn't count as sacrifice.

So, while my batchmates posted pictures in uniforms, I posted photos in formal shirts and MBA badges, pretending my group discussion was a covert operation and Excel formulas were coded battle plans.

Did it hurt? Yes.

Did I sulk? Absolutely.

Did I also eat two samosas in rebellion that day? You bet.

Funny how life reroutes you. One day you're chasing a salute; the next, you're chasing deadlines and hoping your boss doesn't reply "Noted" with a full stop.

Chapter 4

Silver Bells and First Hellos

Before there were sales pitches, LinkedIn bios, or couch-bound commandos, there was Silver Bells. No, not the Christmas carol-though we did sing that too, usually off-key and always off-beat. This Silver Bells was a kindergarten that wasn't so much a school as it was someone's home. Literally.

Silver Bells, run by the ever-graceful Mrs. Saproo, was less of a school and more of a cosy, converted home near IMA's gates. She, along with two other warm-hearted teachers, managed to turn that house into a wonderland for toddlers.

There were no uniforms, no morning assemblies, no bells-just a wild swirl of colourful mats, alphabet posters hanging on by tape and hope, and the unmistakable scent of crayons, glue sticks, and toddler rebellion in the air. We strutted around in outfits that looked like we'd lost a bet with a rainbow-mismatched, glittery, and proud of it. Every day felt like a never-ending birthday party, minus the cake but plus unlimited giggles. The living room had tiny plastic thrones that made us feel like royalty with juice stains, and the backyard boasted a heroic little slide-barely two feet tall, but the way we queued up for our turn, you'd think it was a roller coaster at Disneyland.

Presiding over this pint-sized kingdom of chaos was Mrs. Saproo-our Headmistress, hostess, and honorary grandma rolled into one. She had the gentlest voice, the firmest hands, and a stare that could silence even the loudest lunchbox debate. Alongside her were two other teachers whose names escape me now, but whose ability to juggle flying crayons, snack-time tantrums, and impromptu musical performances deserves lifetime achievement awards.

And then there was Supriya.

Correction-Princess Supriya.

That wasn't a nickname. It was a title. Bestowed by herself. She wore it with the kind of confidence you'd expect from someone with their own kingdom. Whether it was snack time or story time, she made it very clear: she wasn't just any kid-she was royalty. She insisted on being called "Princess" and refused to sit on the same chair twice in a row because, obviously, thrones aren't meant to be reused.

Beside her was Piyush Paul, whose laugh could probably be heard all the way to the IMA parade ground. He had a tiny water bottle that seemed more decorative than functional and a way of losing his shoes without ever noticing. Together, the three of us-Princess, Court Jester, and the Diplomatic Delegate (me, of course)-navigated toddler politics and snack trades with all the seriousness of a cabinet meeting.

But the crown for the most consistently naughty kid? That honor went to Yours Truly.

Now, Mrs. Saproo was a Gandhian at heart-soft-spoken, endlessly patient, a firm believer in non-violence and peaceful conflict resolution. But I tested that ideology so thoroughly, I may have accidentally turned her into a follower of the Subhash Chandra Bose School of Discipline-"Tum mujhe alphabet do, main tumhe punishment dunga."

See, while the class was learning A for Apple, I was insisting on *1, 2, 3*. And the moment we shifted to numbers, I decided the walls looked like they needed some abstract art. I treated the curriculum like a buffet-pick what I liked, ignore the rest, and always go back for more crayons.

Eventually, peace talks failed. Mrs. Saproo had no choice but to resort to the classic Indian disciplinary tool-"Catch your ears!" And I did, with great dramatic flair, like a toddler who'd just been nominated for Best Performance in a Silent Role.

To this day, I blame that phase for why my right ear is ever-so-slightly bigger than the left. Years of asymmetric self-punishment, my friend. Fashionably lopsided-like all great artists.

Outside the walls of Silver Bells, my kingdom expanded into the tree-lined roads of New Race Course-the kind of serene, green cantonment paradise where peacocks casually crossed the road like they owned the place (because honestly, they did). And parked right at the heart of my little empire stood my most prized possession-my Hero Ranger cycle.

Now, let me be clear: this was no ordinary cycle. This was a mechanical marvel, a wheeled warrior, and arguably the most field-tested piece of non-combat equipment ever seen within the boundaries of the Indian Military Academy. In fact, I'm fairly certain my cycle is still a case study at the IMA. Some say it's tucked away in a top-secret archive titled "Engineering Endurance: The Legend of the Indestructible Ranger."

Why the honor, you ask?

Because of the extremely scientific ways I chose to test it.

There were slope-tests (push it downhill without riding it-just to see if it had natural alignment), gravel-survival drills, and a particularly advanced experiment involving telepathic remote control. The tech was simple-whisper "Go Cycle Go" in your most mystical voice, and off it went. Of course, the turning mechanism relied solely on my own magic spell (possibly powered by Abra ka Dabra, Shaka Laka Boom Boom, or sheer toddler conviction).

Only I had the power to change its direction. Not with the handlebars, obviously-that would've been too boring-but through a combination of yelling commands into the wind and intense squinting.

And yet, through all this, not a single spoke was lost. No puncture, no complaints. It endured me with the patience of a monk and the strength of a tank.

If cycles had emotions, mine deserved a bravery medal.

One fine morning, gripped by a sudden surge of cosmic energy (and possibly a sugar rush from two spoonfuls of Bournvita), I decided it was time the world met its youngest superhero. Superman had arrived in New Race Course, and boy, was he underdressed.

I pulled on my bluest fancy dress underwear over my tiny jeans-because that's obviously how superheroes roll-and tied a towel around my neck like it was stitched by Kryptonian tailors themselves. I even insisted on being addressed only as "Super Aman" for the rest of the day.

And then… I ran.

I ran with arms stretched forward, towel-cape flapping behind me in dramatic slo-mo (in my head, at least), as I zoomed past bushes, potted plants, and mildly amused Army officers on their morning walk. My mission? To test the aerodynamics of capes.

The results were promising-I was almost flying, or so I believed, till Mummy spotted me trying to calculate lift by standing on the third step of the staircase and whispering, "Just a little higher and I can take off…"

Thank God I didn't try the terrace.

Somewhere, I'm pretty sure the laws of physics took a deep breath and said, "Not today."

Of course, Superman wasn't my only alter ego. There was also a brief-but unforgettable-Spiderman phase. Inspired by one late-night cartoon binge and one too many Maggi-fueled hallucinations, I became utterly convinced that all I needed was the right wall and the right attitude. Web-shooters? Mere technicalities.

I found the perfect tree near the backyard fence-an innocent, unsuspecting guava tree that clearly hadn't signed up for this nonsense. I climbed halfway up, struck my best Spidey pose, and launched myself off a branch with the full confidence of a boy who believed gravity was just a suggestion.

Needless to say, gravity responded immediately.

I crash-landed into a bush, narrowly missing a flower pot and my dignity. The guava tree survived. The pot survived. I... walked away with a heroic scrape on my elbow that, to this day, remains as a permanent reminder of my superhero career cut tragically short.

Even now, when someone asks about that scar on my elbow, I smile and say, "That? Oh, just a minor injury during my time in the Marvel Universe."

Chapter 5

"Homes in Transit"

The best part of army life? Hands down-postings. New cities, new friends, new schools, new adventures. Every posting felt like life was tossing me into a treasure hunt with no map but endless surprises. And the most underrated thrill of it all? Packing. While the adults sorted logistics and checked lists, I watched our house slowly turn into what looked like a mini railway station. Black wooden boxes lined the hallway like waiting coaches, each stenciled with Papa's name in white paint-as official and mysterious as secret military cargo. For a five-year-old, this was peak entertainment. I'd hop from one box to another like I was catching moving trains, sometimes with friends joining in on the 'station drama.' Mummy, of course, played the ever-alert station master-shooing us away before someone cracked a tooth or an elbow. But for us, it wasn't chaos. It was an adventure, right there in our living room.

Evenings during postings were like a rolling calendar of dinner invitations. We'd head over to homes filled with familiar laughter-Papa and Mummy's friends, and of course, their kids who were my partners-in-crime by default. The grown-ups caught up over endless conversations while we kids turned living rooms into race tracks. But the real excitement always came at the end-when a parting gift was handed to Mummy, wrapped neatly, often with a ribbon that looked way too fancy to stay tied for long.

Now, technically it was Mummy's gift. But practically? Mine. I'd snatch it up with both hands and hold it like it was the crown jewels. Every fibre of my being wanted to rip it open right there, on their sofa, preferably with everyone watching. But then came the look. That one, silent glance from Mummy that said-Not now. Don't even think about it. And just like that, the ribbon survived another hour. Honestly, I still believe all Indian mothers attend a secret "Eyes Only" training camp. One glance and we'd behave like diplomats.

And then came the Big Day-when the truck finally rumbled up to our gate and the entire house buzzed like a movie set about to roll. Our life got packed into it, box by box, with the kind of orchestration that could give a parade a run for its money. I stood there, eyes wide, heart thumping, as the helpers huffed and puffed, shouting over each other while trying to load our fridge like it was an astronaut about to launch into space. The thud it made on the ramp still echoes in my ears-it was pure drama.

And then came the cycle. My cycle. It was practically a celebrity by now-handled with hushed awe, like it had magical powers (which it kind of did, if you count its ability to survive all my experiments). I watched it disappear into the belly of the truck, whispering a silent promise to reunite soon.

"Box number 27-Fragile!" I shouted, half-warning, half-bragging. That one carried my superhero mug-the most precious gift from my favorite teacher. And Box number 6? That had my building blocks and books. I'd insisted on that number because it matched my birthday. Mummy tried to convince me numbers didn't matter. But come on, everyone knows birthday logic always wins.

It was noisy, it was messy, and it was the most thrilling farewell a five-year-old could ask for.

But the real thrill? The train journey.

We'd pile into our first-class coupe-two of three suitcases, a couple of bulging bags, and a legendary picnic basket packed by Mummy, bursting with delicious possibilities. There was always Puri-Aloo (my all-time favourite), a tiny jar of mango pickle, sandwiches , my favourite Kurkure, juicy oranges, and the ever-loyal Parle-G biscuits that, in my humble opinion, deserved national treasure status. And then there was that homemade cake-no one knew when it would appear, but Mummy always pulled it out like a magician's final trick, just when we thought the feast was over.

I'd park myself next to Papa, legs too short to touch the floor, happily swinging while I glued my nose to the window-trying to decode passing mustard fields, count electric poles like a mathematical ninja, and spot imaginary creatures in the clouds. My tiny backpack held all my prized possessions: a drawing book, crayons, a storybook or two, and a superhero sticker collection I guarded like state secrets.

But the best part of it all? Time with Papa. No office, no calls-just us. We told stories, solved riddles, played thumb wars with championship-level seriousness, and sometimes even pretended that our coupe was a secret spaceship on a top mission across the galaxy.

If magic had a sound, I'm convinced it would be that soft, rhythmic clack-clack of the train at night, gently rocking us to sleep while the stars kept pace just outside the window.

And then there was the unofficial best part of every train journey-chai.

The moment the train slowed down near a station, you'd hear that unmistakable call echoing down the platform: "Chaiii… chaiii… garam chaiii!" Like clockwork, the entire compartment would stir. Mummy would smile, Papa would stretch, and I'd sit up straighter-because I knew what was coming.

That steaming plastic glass of railway chai was no ordinary beverage. It was grown-up gold. And the real treat? I was allowed to dip my Parle-G into it.

Just one dip. Two if Mummy looked away.

That moment-soggy biscuit, warm tea, the platform buzzing with movement-felt like a rite of passage. A silent nod from the universe that I was growing up. Of course, I wasn't allowed a full sip of chai… but every now and then, Mummy would pass the glass my way, and I'd steal a tiny, proud sip. Honestly, it felt like being knighted.

Who knew a little glass of tea could taste like freedom?

As the years rolled on, so did we. With each move, the boxes looked a little more worn, the edges frayed from a life well-travelled. My cycle had grown too-newer, shinier, yet already bearing its share of battle scars from wild turns and unfinished stunts. By now, I was a seasoned 'posting child'-well-versed in farewells, bubble wrap, and the sacred art of truck Tetris.

This time, I wasn't just a curious bystander. I had real opinions-about which boxes should go first, which ones needed extra tape, and which ones were definitely mine (even if they technically weren't). I proudly helped Papa seal the cardboard boxes, though most of the time I ended up tangled in brown tape, dramatically yelling "Scissors!" every ten minutes.

Apoorva, our little explorer, had started expressing herself in her own beautiful way-through slurred words, hand gestures, and that unmistakable twinkle in her eye. She didn't need full sentences to be understood; one look, one sound, and we knew-usually that it was snack time again. I took my new title-"elder brother"-with surprising seriousness. I helped carry her sipper, entertained her during long waits, and alerted Mummy every time she tried to climb the sofa like a mountain goat. That, of course, made me feel extremely important.

The journey to Belgaum was on four wheels this time-a long, slightly bumpy drive through some of the most beautiful landscapes I'd ever seen. Endless stretches of greenery rolled past us like scenes from a painting, with clouds brushing the hilltops and fields swaying in the wind. It was the kind of road trip where even the trees seemed to wave goodbye.

We love music-so a drive, for us, *meant* music.

Mummy had her favourite cassette playlist on-Lata Mangeshkar, Kishore Kumar, Jagjit Singh, and a few soulful ghazals that made her hum with a faraway smile. Papa, of course, balanced it out with his classics-the Carpenters, Jim Reeves, Perry Como, Englebert Humperdinck-And me? I was beginning to form my own playlist-Enrique Iglesias, Backstreet Boys, and whatever else made my head nod and heart feel things. My little stash of cassettes may have been smaller, but in that backseat concert hall, it was growing louder.

Apoorva and I claimed the back seat like it was our private lounge-complete with pillows, a comforter, and a fortress of snacks. Mummy had packed our standard journey survival kit: puri, aloo, and that legendary mango pickle that could lift moods and awaken appetites. There was also the usual contraband-Kurkure, chips, and a packet of Parle-G and Bourbon biscuits that somehow vanished faster than we could say "Who ate them?"

I came armed with my own entertainment arsenal-Tinkle, Chacha Chaudhary, and Asterix comics, a deck of UNO cards capable of triggering full-blown sibling diplomacy breakdowns, and a Ludo set that had seen more plot twists than most TV serials.

We rolled into Belgaum with dust in our hair, crumbs on our clothes, and a suitcase full of road trip legends that would be retold at dinner tables for years-each time with a little extra spice. Our first stop was the officers' mess-a polished, no-nonsense kind of place where even the walls seemed to stand at attention and napkins had better posture than us.

But soon, we upgraded to a place we could call home. Curtains went up, boxes were unpacked with dramatic flair, and the unmistakable aroma of Mummy's rajma began marking its territory room by room-like a delicious housewarming ambassador.

Just when the books had found their shelf, the cycle had discovered its new parking nook, and Apoorva had staked claim on every drawer she could reach… the next move started creeping up like a surprise test we all saw coming.

This time, the road led to Delhi.

By now, I didn't just recognize the rhythm of truck loading-I practically choreographed to it. Each thud, scrape, or shuffle was music to my well-trained ears. I could tell which box held books, which one had Mummy's spice tins, and which one absolutely must not be stacked upside down-mostly by how Mummy hovered nearby with arms crossed, eyebrows doing all the talking.

Delhi came with a blast of colder mornings and a much flashier vibe-full-on Punjabi energy with louder horns, brighter weddings, and butter-laced everything.

I wasn't a full-blown teenager yet, but I was on the brink-old enough to roll my eyes, but still young enough to believe that Puri-Aloo was the ultimate travel food. Some things don't change. Neither did our snack squad-Kurkure, chips, Parle-G, and the legendary Bourbon biscuits. Loyalty ran deep.

We didn't just travel with luggage. We traveled with rituals.

With every posting, life subtly shifted. It wasn't just cities that changed-it was us. The way we packed, the way we adjusted our clocks, our tastes, our tone. Each move added something to us, smoothed something else out.

Living out of boxes doesn't just teach you to let go. It teaches you to understand space-your own and others'. It teaches you that home isn't in walls or wallpaper but in warmth, resilience, and how you adapt when the scenery changes.

Somewhere between farewells and fresh starts, I grew. Slowly, without announcement.

I learned to read people the way I once read comic books-looking for the story behind their words. I learned to wait, to listen, to accommodate different ways of speaking, dressing, living. And I began to understand that the more places you've lived in, the more places live in you.

Every city left its fingerprint-on the way I spoke, the things I craved, the jokes I laughed at, even the pauses I grew comfortable with. Over time, I realised-I wasn't just passing through these places. They were passing through me too, shaping how I saw the world and how gently I began to hold it.

And through it all, what truly shaped me wasn't the destination.

It was the journey.

Soon after came our final school-life move-Chandimandir.

By now, I didn't just dip Parle-G in chai-I sipped it while reading books, curating CD playlists, or scribbling into a half-filled travel journal that smelled faintly of biscuit crumbs and ink. My music had grown louder, deeper, and unapologetically mine. Pink Floyd's echoing questions, Metallica's rage, Guns N' Roses' drama, Nirvana's chaos-they all made sense in their own strange way. Somewhere between solos and silent highways, I was discovering the rhythm of my own thoughts.

The boy who once chased dragonflies in Mhow-and ended up with stitches across his belly and a cautionary tale for every picnic-was now the one refreshing weather reports before journeys, quietly deciding which CD deserved the stereo first. I'd grown up, yes. But not just because of the ticking clock or the changing pin codes.

Some growth doesn't come with a loud announcement. It arrives in silence-in long hospital nights, in watching your younger sister, Apoorva, face life with cerebral palsy and still manage to light up every room. Loving her, growing up beside her, taught me a kind of strength that isn't loud. It taught me to listen more, to judge less, to be still when needed, and to hold space for what cannot be fixed.

Maybe it was the ache stitched into my own body that taught me resilience. Or maybe it was watching her quietly push through everyday challenges with grit and grace that gave me perspective. Somewhere between her soft laughter and my posters of rock bands, something shifted.

I began to understand that strength isn't always physical, that courage often looks like getting up again, and that empathy is a form of wisdom. Maybe those stitches on my stomach had sewn in some maturity too-less visible, but lasting.

Still, I hadn't lost all the sparkle. I'd pout if Papa picked his collection over my Pink Floyd. I still carried UNO cards like they were emergency gear. And I still believed, stubbornly, that mango pickle and music could fix almost anything.

Anyway, let's get rolling. After all that heavy stuff, don't go thinking I turned into some saint-in-school-uniform.

My jokes were sharper now, my playlists moodier , but my eyes still lit up at the sound of wheels on gravel and the scent of Mummy's travel snacks wafting through the car.

The magic of postings? That hadn't changed.

Because no matter how tall I got or how many cities we ticked off, some things stayed delightfully constant-Papa's debates with Maps, Apoorva's giggles mid-traffic, Mummy's uncanny ability to pull out napkins, pain balms, or snacks like a magician with a bottomless handbag.

Every goodbye left a tiny ache. Every new beginning brought butterflies and new school uniforms. But that was the beauty of it-we weren't just adjusting to places. We were absorbing them. Collecting little bits of every city, every home, every laugh.

Because home was never a postal pin.

It was wherever the four of us went next.

Chapter 6

"Benchmates & Break Times"

Before life came with passwords and PowerPoint decks, it came with lunchboxes overflowing with Mummy's love-stuffed parathas, aloo rolls, or whatever tasted like home, half-chewed pencil tops, scraped knees, and that one loyal bench that held your back, your secrets, and your carved initials.

School wasn't just where we went to "study." Please. It was where we lived. Between the ringing bells and whispered roll calls, we built empires out of chalk pieces, declared war with paper balls, and survived the daily battlefield called PT period, where running was optional but dramatic excuses were not.

Friendships back then weren't about shared playlists or mutual follows. They were born over borrowed erasers, double lunchbox diplomacy, and silent pacts sealed with a glance during surprise tests. These weren't friends you scrolled to find-they showed up somewhere between Mummy's parathas, missing chalk, and the kind of laughter that got you thrown out of class together.

And that bench? It wasn't just a piece of wood- it was everything. A courtroom for dramatic betrayals ('You told her I like her?!'), a confession box for crushes and cribs, a comedy club with questionable jokes, and once, a full-blown hospital ward after an overambitious football tackle that ended in a heroic limp and a lot of Dettol.

This Chapter isn't about academics-don't worry, I won't make you solve a math problem.

This is about the beautiful, glorious mess of school days. The friends we met, the rules we bent, and the memories that still smell faintly of Fevicol and samosas.

But every legendary school story needs a starting point.

And mine? It began in Mhow.

A sleepy little cantonment where mornings smelt like wet earth and chalk dust, and afternoons melted into a golden haze of PT drills and paratha-fuelled laughter. If school life was a movie, then Mhow was my opening montage-sunlight dancing through tree-lined streets, polished black shoes kicking up red dust, and the background score? A mash-up of assembly prayers, bell gongs, and the occasional whistle from a PT sir who thought he was training us for the Olympics.

If Army postings were treasure maps, then Mhow was that bright, cheerful X that didn't scream for attention-it simply smiled, calm and quiet, as if it knew you'd fall in love with it... slowly, then all at once. It was all there-open fields, playgrounds, neighbours who knew your name (and your lunchbox contents), and a peaceful stillness that wrapped around your world like a familiar quilt.

And right in the heart of it all stood Army Public School, Mhow-my first real universe of scraped knees, inside jokes, and friendships that felt more permanent than anything written in ink.

That's where I met Mayuk, Riya, and Divya Kirti-my first little crew. Riya had a sharp tongue and sharper brains, Divya Kirti was the quiet genius who probably noticed things even our teacher didn't, and Mayuk had this unwavering confidence in his half-baked facts. But together, we just... worked. Like pencils and sharpener caps-forever getting lost, but somehow always found together.

You know how every cartoon gang has the talker, the thinker, the dreamer, and the one cooking up wild ideas in the background? That was us. We weren't exactly solving mysteries, but we sure were creating enough of them.

We didn't just attend school. We occupied it.

Together, we were unstoppable.

Think one part mischief, two parts wild imagination, and just enough drama to earn us unofficial status as "case studies" in teacher gossip circles-usually whispered over chai and headache pills.

There were no real rules that couldn't be bent, and no corners of the school we didn't poke our noses into. By the end of lunch break, our classroom looked like Washing Powder Nirma needed to send in reinforcements. Chalk dust everywhere, paper planes, erasers that had gone AWOL, and at least one grand water spill under someone's desk resembling a mini Yamuna in full flood.

Our class teacher would walk in, take a dramatic pause, scan the room like a crime scene investigator, and go, "Who did this?!"

We'd sit there like monks in meditation-halo over our heads, hands folded on the desk. Not a single movement, not a whisper. Our gang had an unspoken pact of silence, unless Karan (the self-declared assistant to the teacher) decided to switch careers to detective and blow our cover.

But that's the thing about early friendships. They weren't built on status updates or story replies. They were forged over shared tiffins, failed whisper games, and alliances like, "If we're caught, we go down together."

Next stop? An all-boys school that wasn't the strict, gray kind you see in movies. No cold echoing hallways or scary headmasters with monocles-this place had soul. The kind of quiet, timeless charm you usually find in Ruskin Bond stories. Think arched corridors, red-tiled roofs, and classrooms that smelt faintly of chalk, ambition, and old wooden desks with names carved deeper than the syllabus ever went.

Set in a sleepy corner of Belgaum where time moved at its own pace, the school was less of an institution and more of an atmosphere. A place where the bell didn't just signal change of periods-it triggered football rivalries, tiffin negotiations, and last-minute homework scribbles.

This was St. Paul's. And if you ever studied there, you'll know exactly what I mean.

Thanks to my stomach injury, I wasn't much of a sports guy anymore-but that didn't mean I faded into the background. Dramatics, fancy dress competitions, chorus singing, and school band performances? Count me in. That stage was my stadium. I was always ready to recite the "Thought for the Day"- so much so, if anyone developed cold feet or backed out because of stage fright or simply decided to be absent, I was always the standby speaker.

I made some solid friends-Gaurav and Amog were my closest, along with Joel (the only one who could sing better than me and knew it), Pradyumna (who swore he'd be an IPS officer someday and already walked like one), and Nikhil (the quiet observer who always carried two pens and a packet of mints for no reason at all).

After school, we'd head straight to Mama's shop-that magical little place that had everything from compass boxes to chewing gum, stickers, to spicy samosas. If Hogwarts had Honeydukes, we had Mama's.

This was also the year of the pen. Goodbye pencils-this was when we graduated to using ink. And boy, did it matter. I was obsessed with pens-especially the Parker ones. Way too expensive for a kid, but just holding one made you feel like a CEO in training.

Even if I didn't have one, I'd stare at the display like it was an Oscar trophy. There was something about the weight of it in your hand. You weren't just writing-you were authoring your legacy. Even if it was just cursive writing practice.

After my St. Paul's adventure, I found myself stepping into a school that was more than just a new campus-it was personal. Tucked inside Belgaum's peaceful curves was a world with a quiet, old-school charm. The kind you don't just attend, but inherit.

This Military School wasn't just run by the Army-it was practically etched into my father's DNA. He had once sat on those very benches as a young cadet, and now, years later, returned as the Principal. For Papa, it wasn't just the best school in the world-it *was* the world. And thanks to him, I didn't just join the school... I joined the legacy.

Red-tiled roofs that glowed like embers at dusk, breezy corridors that carried echoes of shared secrets, and classrooms where stories unfolded one bell at a time. It was a Military School, yes-but not the kind with bugles and barked orders. Picture khaki shirts, matching shorts, and sunshine pooling in every open courtyard. The boys weren't just classmates-they were cadets, roommates, co-conspirators. An accidental family forged by routine, rivalry, and the kind of laughter that only comes from eating, sleeping, studying, and growing up together.

We didn't just live near the school-we lived *within* its heartbeat. This wasn't your typical school with the usual morning rush and parents honking outside the gate.

This was a proper Military School, nestled in the quiet embrace of Belgaum, where discipline wasn't drilled in-it was simply part of the atmosphere.

Here, the Indian Army wasn't just a symbol on the school crest-it was the very spine of the place. Run by serving officers, the school carried itself with quiet pride. The kind that didn't need to shout to command respect. Mornings weren't chaotic-they were clockwork. The sun always seemed to rise on time, and so did we.

While the cadets stayed in long rows of hostels across campus, our house stood in one peaceful corner. My father-who had once stood in formation here as a cadet-had now returned in olive green; this time as the Principal. The pride he carried for the school was impossible to miss. For him, it wasn't just a posting-it was an emotional homecoming. For me? It was part legacy, part constant surveillance.

Because when your dad runs the show, you don't exactly slip under the radar. You *are* the radar. Everyone knew your name, your roll number, who dropped by your house on Sunday, what you scored in last week's test, and exactly how many times your mum yelled your name from the living room -it wasn't a VIP pass. It was more like walking around with a neon sign over my head that blinked "PRINCIPAL'S SON-OBSERVE CLOSELY."

While most boys had the luxury of getting caught only once in a while, I had teachers, seniors, and Papa keeping track like *I was a live mission*.

So I did what any self-respecting, permanently-under-the-spotlight kid would do-I grabbed the mic and ran with it. If there was a stage, I was on it. Elocution? Check. Chorus singing? Absolutely. Dramatics? Bring it on. At 8 AM, while the rest of the school was still digesting their dreams, I'd be dramatically declaring, *"Half a league, half a league…"*, like I was leading the cavalry charge myself.

Somewhere between the applause and the eye-rolls from sleepy classmates, the stage stopped being a spotlight-it became home. A place where I wasn't just the Principal's kid. I was me, in full theatrical surround sound.

Sure, I ate most meals at home (a luxury that my taste buds never took for granted), the rest of my time was shoulder-to-shoulder with the boys. We played together, marched together.

Group activities where "teamwork" usually meant doing all the work because your buddy had "a mild fever." Shared punishments that bonded us better than friendship bracelets, and inside jokes that could still crack us up mid-meeting, years later.

In a world of identical khaki uniforms, synchronized marching, and emotional support during math tests, those boys weren't just classmates-they were brothers-in-arms. No rifles, of course, but a whole lot of attitude, sweaty handshakes, and a silent agreement that whoever fell asleep first during prep would get doodled on with a blue pen.

The best part about being classmates with the Principal's son? Let's just say it came with edible perks. And because it was Papa's school-his *Alma Mater*, his pride, his temple-the pampering wasn't just for my classmates. Oh no, the entire school soaked in that emotional spotlight like uniforms drying in the Belgaum sun.

Picnics? We didn't just get a bus and soggy sandwiches-we got DJ speakers, gulab jamuns that kept magically appearing, and enough snacks to trigger a strategic sugar high. Holi parties? Buckets of colour, a full-blown food fest, and group photos where half the cadets looked like they'd been through a rainbow explosion-and loved every second of it. Diwali? The whole school lit up like someone gave the fairy lights a promotion. Sweets flowed freely, and even the mess staff smiled like they had cracked NDA.

No one asked why things were extra festive. Everyone just knew-when the Principal loves the school like it's his first-born, you don't just celebrate festivals... you upgrade them.

You see, when Papa called it "my school," he didn't just mean his office or the Principal's chair. He meant every brick, every kid, every silly group song belted out of tune in the assembly hall. We didn't just attend school-we were part of its extended family, complete with occasional homemade laddoos and lifelong memories.

I made some great friends there-Gaurav, Amog, Vaibhav. The kind of friends who'd fight with me over a broken pen cap but stand beside me like bodyguards during surprise inspections. The senior boys-Shailender, Arun-took me under their wing like I was their little sidekick… or maybe their unpaid intern. Either way, I was in.

I threw myself into school life, and school life didn't just accept me-it gave me a bear hug and a few harmless bruises. Military School didn't just teach me how to march in straight lines; it taught me how to take feedback without flinching, how to speak up without shouting, and how to adjust my personality without shrinking it. I learnt that real leadership sometimes meant cleaning up after your team-not just directing them.

I only stayed till Class 6, but it left a mark deeper than any House badge. It wasn't just about medals or morning drills-it was about empathy. I began to understand that while we all wore the same uniform, everyone carried different battles. That sometimes, the loudest kid needed a friend, not a warning.

That quiet emotional intelligence? It stuck with me. Helped me years later during MBA group projects where some people confused PowerPoint animations with leadership.

And yes, I still straighten my bedsheet in one go. Old habits-and Army influence-die hard.

After Belgaum, I graduated to Bangalore Military School-this time as a full-fledged boarder. No going home for lunch, no mummy around the corner-just me, my trunk, and a bunch of boys who snored like tractors and laughed like hyenas. For me, it was less of a school and more of a long-awaited slumber party… with uniforms, PT, and suspiciously identical haircuts.

But just when I started enjoying the brotherhood-the midnight whispers, the mess food negotiations, the who-stole-my-toothpaste mysteries-my digestive system decided to stage a rebellion. Old abdominal war wounds from my childhood accident came back for a sequel. Apparently, my intestines had their own opinions about hostel life and my stomach, dramatic as always, decided that hostel sambhar wasn't its idea of fine dining. It clearly hadn't signed up for a South Indian menu.

So, within six or seven months, I had to wrap up my boarding school dreams. Disappointed? Sure. But even in that short stay, I had a blast. Living with boys who felt like brothers, sharing secrets, and collecting enough inside jokes to last a lifetime-Bangalore left a stamp on my heart (and a few on my digestive tract).

Funny how life works. Years later, Bangalore would come calling again-this time not with khaki shorts, but with corporate suits and another round of North-South negotiations. But we'll get to that soon.

If Belgaum was where discipline first shook my hand, then Army Public School, Dhaula Kuan was where mischief slapped me on the back and said, "Welcome to teenage."

This was the age of voice cracks, awkward confidence, and the golden discovery that chewing gum had more uses than advertised-like being expertly stuck under desks, chairs, and once, horrifyingly, a teacher's dupatta.

My gang? Oh, we were a total ensemble cast. Vinamrata, Vibha, Prashant Bhardwaj (who went on to join the Army-Sikh Regiment, if my memory serves me right), and the occasional guest appearance by Namrata Dalal. We weren't just classmates; we were a full-blown teenage soap opera-complete with shifting group dynamics, dramatic "I'm never talking to you again" declarations, and reconciliations over patties at the canteen 37 minutes later.

We're still connected, still rooting for each other. They're all doing brilliantly, and I'm genuinely proud of them. Vinamrata is in Chandigarh, and whenever I'm back home, catching up with her is a given-like clockwork, or like mom's aloo paratha on Sundays. Honestly, these friends probably know me better than I know myself.

And yes... there were teenage crushes. Silly secrets. The kind of innocent love stories that never made it to the yearbook but still manage to sneak into your thoughts when you least expect it. The stuff that makes nostalgia taste like softy ice cream from the school gate-sweet, slightly messy, and totally unforgettable.

Canteen time was sacred. The patties there were the stuff that legends are made of. Golden, flaky, slightly mysterious on the inside, and totally worth selling your geometry box for. Recess meant two things: running to grab a seat before it vanished, and then doing a careful gum inspection of the chairs-because some people believed furniture was a great place to recycle their chewing gum.

Mimicry became our unofficial sport. We'd copy each other's laughs, teachers' quirks, and even the way someone ran to the canteen like it was an Olympic sprint. We were young, borderline annoying, and having the time of our lives.

APS Dhaula Kuan wasn't just another school-it was a livewire Chapter of laughter, rebellion (the harmless kind), and friendships that taught me how to stand my ground and also laugh at myself. Lessons that, weirdly enough, proved just as useful in corporate boardrooms as they did in school corridors.

We were also developing a pretty solid taste in music-mostly rock, some metal, and a whole lot of attitude. In da Club, Linkin Park, Nirvana, Metallica… we weren't just classmates, we were a bunch of 12 or 13-year-olds trying to process life through guitar riffs and hoodie sleeves. We'd exchange lyrics scribbled on notebook margins, debate over which song had the best bridge (as if we knew what a bridge even was), and lend each other scratched CDs like they were family heirlooms.

That's the beautiful thing about growing up in Army circles-you don't need an icebreaker. Everyone's already humming the same track, watching the same movies, or quoting the same Jim Carrey line. The cultural download happens on autopilot. You're new, you bond over a bunk bed, a cricket match, or the shared trauma of mess food, and by lunch break, you're soul siblings.

And honestly? That phase was the ultimate crash course in corporate survival. No business school can prepare you like chasing the last pattie in the canteen while negotiating territorial claims over the bench with three other hungry teenagers. That's not lunch-it's pre-sales training. Convincing a classmate who hadn't opened a book all year to lead the group presentation? That's strategic delegation, bro.

In sales today, it's pretty much the same circus-just shinier. Get the client's attention, fake confidence like you used to fake homework, speak their language ("synergy," not "sup bro"), and close the deal before they ghost. Back then, rejection meant they didn't return your "Do you like me? Tick yes or no" note. Now, it's "We'll get back to you after Q4."

Looking back, those teenage years were the original character-building bootcamp. Honestly, a way better prep for the corporate jungle than any online MBA or a painfully slow PowerPoint workshop. Because let's face it-working in sales is just like being 13 again, but with better shoes and worse knees. Convincing someone to buy a software package is just adult code for: "Dude, seriously, give this band a listen-it'll change your life."

Only now, instead of detention for bunking class, you get a passive-aggressive calendar invite titled "Sync on missed KPIs." And your angsty Linkin Park playlist? It's still there-just playing softly behind an Excel sheet while you adjust pricing strategies and silently scream into your coffee mug.

But that gang, those songs, the ridiculous group fights about who gets to sit next to whom in the canteen-they knew me before I became "Aman who nods seriously while wondering what the client actually wants." They knew the playlist before LinkedIn tried to rebrand me. And trust me, that version of me? Way cooler, slightly louder... and definitely better at air guitar.

These days, that version resurfaces whenever one of our WhatsApp groups lights up. Someone posts a blurry canteen photo, someone else revives an age-old joke, and suddenly, I'm back there-less 'target achiever,' more 'part-time drummer on the desk with pencils.' Corporate life may come with business cards, but school came with punchlines that actually landed.

And then came the next Chapter: Army Public School, Chandimandir.

New set of corridors. New uniforms. New code of survival. This time, I didn't just walk in-I *glided* in with the quiet overconfidence of someone who thought changing schools was a talent. I was the guy who had opinions, playlists, and a growing collection of inside jokes from every pin code we'd lived in.

What began as yet another posting for Papa-this time to Srinagar-suddenly turned into a personal upgrade. Mummy decided to stay back in Panchkula with Apoorva, and I... well, I got promoted.

To what, you ask?

The Man of the House.

In reality? It meant I was suddenly responsible for:

Depositing cheques without accidentally turning them into bookmarks,

Telling the gas delivery guy, "Mummy's not home, but I'm in charge," in a voice that cracked halfway through and made him blink twice,

Strolling into the vegetable shop like a CEO with a mission-only to spend five confused minutes playing Guess That Vegetable.

Was it a papaya or a pumpkin? A watermelon or just a really hydrated kaddu? I wasn't sure, but I brought it home with confidence.

I also didn't understand why medium bhindis were somehow superior to the long ones. I thought bhindi was bhindi, not a personality type.

And of course, I'd often walk out of the store triumphantly-only to realize I'd left two items at the billing counter.

Mummy would ask, "Where are the lemons?" and I'd go sprinting back like it was the 100 m finals.

Somewhere between decoding vegetable hieroglyphics and munching on a Cornetto on the way back (very important for stress relief), I started believing I could handle anything. Even Apoorva's homework.

Yes-sometimes I was her teacher too. Sitting with her, explaining spellings and maths problems like I was running a one-kid coaching centre at home.

And honestly? I think I learned stress management right there. Balancing homework, groceries, forgotten milk packets, and ice cream therapy. No wonder I handle client escalations like a monk on mute.

Just eat ice cream, breathe, and reboot life.

Sure, I still wore a school bag and got told to finish my milk, but now I walked into banks like I was applying for a home loan. I even wore a watch-mostly to check how long I'd survived without adult supervision.

I still remember one proud afternoon when I marched into the bank, chest out, cheque in hand, and asked the teller, "Can I encash this *account*?"

The teller blinked twice, nodded slowly, and probably went home that night with a fantastic dinner table story.

But in some strange, sitcom-like way, these were my first internships in adulting-at just 13, with zero qualifications and unlimited confidence. Those awkward missions-like asking the chemist for medicine I couldn't pronounce or convincing the sabziwala that I definitely knew how much half a kilo of bhindi should cost-were my mini MBA projects.

Each small win, like getting the right change or managing not to leave the milk packet behind at the shop (again), built invisible muscles I didn't even know I'd need.

Today, when I fill out expense reports or lead a client pitch, I draw from those early days of winging it.

Because let's be honest-corporate life is just a more sanitized version of childhood confusion.

Same drama, fancier clothes.

Back then, I was learning to hold it all together when nothing made sense.

Which, now that I think about it, is also the unofficial job description of adulthood.

Add a blazer, hide the panic, and always carry a Cornetto for emergencies.

Anyway...

While I was trying to balance gas bookings and gulab jamuns, something else was cooking-Chandimandir.

New school. New friends. And me, walking in like I was carrying the burden of an empire… in a backpack.

I joined tuition for Maths in 10th grade.

Now, did it improve my calculation skills? Not really.

Did I suddenly start solving equations like a prodigy? Absolutely not.

But did I end up with some solid friendships and even better jokes? Oh, 100%.

Enter: Karan Syal, Nayhel, and Tanush Sangwan-my tuition buddies, my partners-in-chaos, my unofficial brothers in crime.

We're still in touch, and honestly, that's probably the only real takeaway from those evening classes.

We had all the fun at Vaidya Ma'am's tuition.

And when I say fun, I mean the kind of unfiltered, post-school energy that could've powered a small city.

I still don't know how Vaidya Ma'am managed to tolerate our madness.

She had the patience of a saint and the reflexes of a ninja-dodging our random questions, flying paper balls, and "ma'am-bas-5-minute-break" requests like a pro.

To her credit, she never gave up on trying to teach us.

To our credit, we *never* gave up on trying to distract each other with full-volume whispering and snack sneak-ins.

Honestly, Maths was about laughter, snacks, and pretending to understand trigonometry while planning weekend plans.

We would've all topped the board exams-if marks were given for snack smuggling, inside jokes, and creative ways to delay assignments.

After 10th, I chose Commerce.

Business Studies felt like something I could confidently fake till I made it.

Economics had its mood swings, but we managed to stay civil.

And Hindi?

Let's just say-we had a dignified farewell.

We didn't ghost each other.

We sat down like two mature individuals, acknowledged the journey, and mutually decided to go our separate ways.

No regrets. No drama.

Except for that one Chapter that went so off-track, even the teacher gave up halfway and started discussing dal makhani.

So, that's how I entered the glamorous world of debit-credit and invisible supply-demand curves… with a heart free of guilt, and a timetable free of शुद्ध लेखन.

And somewhere between all this-Papa still posted in Srinagar, Mummy multitasking like a superhero, Apoorva being the sunshine of the house-I grew up. Kind of.

Or at least, I started acting like it. With a rock playlist in one ear and an economics doubt in the other.

House Captain material? Apparently.

They gave me the badge. The responsibility. The illusion of power.

Suddenly, I was part of an elite club that said things like,

"Discipline matters!"

and also quietly muttered,

"Wait, where did I keep my own belt?"

My duties? Oh, just the usual superhero stuff:

Yelling "Walk on the left!" while I sprinted to the canteen like Usain Bolt.

Telling 7th graders to tuck their shirts in, even though mine was doing the cha-cha with my belt.

Breaking up imaginary fights that were actually just people arguing over the last samosa.

And carrying that school diary like it was a launch code folder, writing "Names!" with so much authority, you'd think it was the Parliament logbook.

But let's be real-I wasn't running the school.

I was just a glorified traffic cop in Bata shoes, with a badge, a gel pen, and the deep internal conflict of whether to report my friend or just fake-write their name in the air.

Respect? Maybe.

Power? Debatable.

Fun? Absolutely.

Because where else do you get to feel like an HR manager and a Bollywood villain-all before recess?

The Gang.

Sarabvir Singh. Shruti Rawat. Sanam Sekhon. Tanush Sangwan.

By the time you hit Class 10th onwards, friendships aren't made-they're just... forged. Usually in the heat of group assignments, birthday party planning, or collectively failing to finish assignments.

We weren't perfect.

We had full-blown arguments over birthday party themes, group project credits, and who stole whose Parker pen.

But despite the drama, the teasing, the tiny Cold Wars, we were solid.

One sarcastic line.

One shared eye-roll during a never-ending lecture.

Boom-back to being inseparable.

We fought like siblings. We covered for each other like partners-in-crime.

And when the canteen bhaiya announced, "Only one pattie left,"-we teamed up like Avengers on a carb mission.

Then came Orkut. Yahoo Messenger. Those long "last seen at" debates.

And just when we thought we couldn't talk more... Facebook happened.

Followed by phones with polyphonic ringtones and Snake II.

Obviously, the connection only got stronger.

Today, we may be scattered across time zones, jobs, and parenting struggles,

but one badly cropped throwback photo or an old prank resurfaces on the group chat-

and just like that, we're fifteen again.

Because some friendships don't fade.

They just get better Wi-Fi.

As Karan Johar launches all the star kids, I too had a bit of… let's call it "infrastructure support."

Papa's good friend, our Principal-Col. Babbarwal Sir-made sure I was well looked after. Well-fed, well-watched, and *mildly feared*.

Yes, dear reader, even school had nepotism.

And honestly? I believe people only complain about it when they don't get access.

Just saying.

Jokes apart, growing up in a familiar environment does give you a kind of invisible safety net. But let's not forget-the net came with CCTV-level surveillance.

One late arrival, one canteen argument, or one "accidentally-forgotten" homework sheet-and the news reached home before I did.

My school bag didn't carry books. It carried evidence.

It had its perks:

You were nurtured, noticed, and could never completely lose your way.

But the flip side?

You couldn't fake a stomach ache without someone reporting your samosa sighting in the canteen.

Honestly, sometimes I wish I had one Col. Babbarwal Sir in my corporate life too.

Just sitting there in a control room with a walkie-talkie whispering:

"Aman. Don't CC the wrong client.

And for the love of God, your Excel sheet has 3 hidden columns-again."

But here I am.

All grown up, making decisions.

No backup. No Col Babbarwal Sir. Just Wi-Fi and wishful thinking.

Let's be real-most of my early decisions weren't Chanakya-level wise.

They were more like freestyle improve: part gut instinct, part panic, part "let's see what happens."

Because I wasn't the kind to learn from other people's mistakes.

No, no-I curated my own. With full dedication and originality.

Every blunder had a signature.

But hey, I survived.

And now I have a solid collection of stories, life lessons, and… some permanent Excel trauma.

Because some people learn through books.

Some through mentors.

And some of us… through fire drills, billing errors, and proudly clicking "Reply All" by mistake.

Right around then, life got its first serious upgrade-

Enter: my first mobile phone. The iconic Nokia.

Small enough to fit in your palm, strong enough to survive a fall from the second floor, and humble enough to offer just calls, SMS, and the great Snake II.

No camera, no apps, no swiping-just plain old texting with a keypad that required finger stamina and predictive T9 skills.

Typing "what's up?" felt like doing cardio for your thumbs.

But suddenly, friendships weren't confined to school hours anymore.

They extended into the night, through missed calls (read: "call me back, I have no balance"), long message threads, and emotional Orkut testimonials like:

"U r d bsttt brooo"

Back then, one incoming message could cause full-blown excitement-especially if it vibrated during class.

(And we all had that one friend who'd reply only with "k." Yes, we're still friends. Barely.)

Mobile phones weren't just gadgets. They were social status.

And that Nokia-despite its pixelated charm-was the badge of entry into after-school gossip, planning

SOI (Shivalik Officer's Institute) parties, or just texting "Good Night" to 17 people… and waiting for replies like your emotional wellbeing depended on it.

It wasn't about features. It was about freedom.

The joy of calling your friend after school even though you just spent 7 hours with them.

Or pretending to be busy on a call when your crush walked by. (Guilty.)

Those were the pre-smartphone, full-heart days-

Where friendships lived in inbox folders, battery bars were sacred, and one SMS could turn your whole day around.

The best part of studying in an Army school?

Your friends are basically part of your extended Army family.

The worst part?

Your crushes are part of that same family.

It's like growing up in a giant surveillance state… but with polished shoes and morning assembly.

See, in most schools, if a guy liked a girl, he could just… you know, say it. Maybe pass a note. Drop a hint. Slide into her Yahoo Messenger.

But not us.

We were soldiers' kids.

If I even thought a girl was cute, chances were-her dad and my dad had served in the same unit.

Which basically made us cousins by uniform. Romantic disaster.

Worse, the moment you even looked at someone for 0.2 seconds longer than normal,

some "well-meaning" friend would go,

"Ayyyye, Aman likes her!"

loud enough for the entire Parade Ground to hear.

And you'd be standing there like-

"No, no! I was just checking if her tie was… aligned! I swear!"

Because once word got out, it would travel faster than an Army wireless message:

from canteen → to staff room → to your mom's ladies group → to your dad over dinner.

By 8:00 PM, you were getting a career counseling lecture for falling in love at 16.

So we all became experts in undercover emotions.

Code names, inside jokes, and those awkward sideways glances.

Our idea of flirting?

"Hey, I saved you a seat on the school bus."

Translation: I might actually marry you one day, but also, please don't tell your dad, because he's my papa's friend.

Looking back, I realize-

romance in Army school wasn't Bollywood.

It was more like Mission Impossible.

By the way, as I was evolving, so was my playlist.

Screaming guitars, angsty lyrics, and hypnotic instrumentals that made you feel things-even if you had no idea what exactly you were feeling.

My go-to soundtrack was basically a rock museum:

Aerosmith, Led Zeppelin, The Cars, The Rolling Stones, Eagles' "Already Gone," Fastway's "Say What You Will," 38 Special's "If I'd Been the One," and Billy Squier's "In the Dark."

What was I even processing back then?

Academic confusion? → *"Comfortably Numb."*

(Because honestly, I still don't know how I cleared Class 12. Maybe the examiner just caught the vibe and went, "Bless this poor confused soul.")

Heartbroken? Existential? Or just hungry again? Hard to say.

At some point, I even started enjoying instrumentals-no lyrics, just pure vibes.

Maybe it was all the teenage drama.

Or maybe because music without words made more sense than half the conversations I was having at 16.

While everyone else was busy picking subjects, I was out there curating playlists for emotions I hadn't even named yet.

Feeling mysterious for no reason? → Anything by Floyd with a 7-minute intro and zero chorus.

Basically, music became my therapist, my escape room, and my rebellion-all rolled into one.

No appointments. Just decent headphones and no nosy relatives around.

So yeah, school life wrapped up with guitar solos, half-filled notebooks, and surprisingly decent grades.

I wasn't the best, but I was the best at surviving. That counts.

And just like that-cue graduation music-I moved on from Army School to DAV College, Chandigarh.

College life officially began the day I got my bus pass.

Not an ID card. Not a timetable.

Just that laminated rectangle of hope that said:

"Congratulations, you're still not getting a bike."

See, I was accident-prone royalty.

Convincing Mummy to let me ride a bike was like trying to convince the Indian government to cancel tea time.

Her logic? Flawless:

"You don't need a bike. You need blessings. And maybe bubble wrap."

So while my classmates zoomed around in open jeeps and shiny hatchbacks blasting Yo Yo Honey Singh,

I boarded the local bus like a grounded rockstar.

Window seat. Bag on lap. And dreams slightly delayed.

Welcome to DAV Chandigarh-where education was optional, but learning life? That was compulsory.

First thing I did after landing in DAV Chandigarh?

Step one in my personal growth plan!

Join "Aaghaaz"-the college dramatics society.

Because obviously, Ayushmann Khurrana had done it.

And I too believed I had the range.

The voice. The stage presence. The unnecessary hand movements.

So I strutted in like it was my personal biopic-

Eyes full of dreams. Shirt slightly unbuttoned.

And a practiced pause after every sentence. (Because theatre, bro.)

But just as I was about to deliver my monologue-poof-the lights went out.

Power failure?

Nope.

Apparently, I was "illuminating" too much.

Their exact words:

"Thank you, dear… We'll first work on our skills and then dare to perform beside someone of your Hollywood caliber."

I was flattered.

Also mildly confused.

Was it praise or a gentle audition exit strategy disguised as poetry?

But you know what? I took it.

Because in my head, that day, I was too good for the grid.

Stage couldn't handle my wattage.

Chandigarh wasn't ready for this level of theatrical glow.

I had out-Ayushmanned Ayushmann.

So I walked out, head held high, like a misunderstood star who'd one day tell this story on Koffee with Karan.

(Just without the coffee. Or Karan. Or the couch.)

Still, that day taught me two things:

Every college society has drama-even before the rehearsals start.

Always carry a torch in Chandigarh. Especially if your charisma is a fire hazard.

Meanwhile, real theatre was happening daily-in the canteen.

DAV had its own Punjabi pulse-loud, proud, and dripping in swag.

The parking lot looked like a car expo: Scorpios, Swifts, and speakers that could wake your ancestors.

Fashion was an extreme sport.

Confidence was served with extra cologne.

And the canteen?

Oh, the canteen.

Butter chicken, butter naan, and a side of Domino's.

Because nothing says college lunch like Punjabi cuisine flirting with global franchises.

My crew?

Harinder (we called him Harry, even though he looked nothing like Potter),

Gurpreet (aka GPS, because he always knew where the next party was),

Parvinder, Charanjeet, and Sukhbir-each one louder and funnier than the last.

Together, we formed an elite squad of Canteen Critics & Gedi Experts.

Our HQ?

Nik Baker's, Sector 9.

For a guy without a bike, I was suspiciously good at splurging on overpriced pastries.

And when we weren't debating over who'd foot the bill,

we were out on the Gedi Route-windows down, music loud,

driving in circles with no destination like philosophical Ferraris,

pretending every red light was our Cannes red carpet moment.

College didn't teach me how to do taxes.

But it did teach me how to read a canteen menu like a stockbroker, how to stretch pocket money like a yoga master, and how to survive hangouts, and harsh Chandigarh sun, with a side of humour and Harinder.

Now, don't get me wrong-

I was serious about my studies.

I mean, I wasn't topping the class, but I wasn't tanking it either.

I was that reliable, middle-order batsman-sometimes scoring a fifty, occasionally pulling off a century, but mostly… playing for survival.

But I was equally serious about one more thing-my friends.

And when two of them were in the hostel?

Well, college felt like a sitcom written by a sleep-deprived writer-hilarious, unpredictable, and constantly reusing the same jokes and jeans.

Some days, I'd wake up all fired up-

Today, I'll focus.

No distractions. Just me, my books, and an imaginary vision board taped to my mental wall.

But before I could even whisper "Perfect competition market..."

someone would barge in like they were Maverick in Top Gun, yelling:

"Bro, we're heading out for a lassi round. Notes can wait!"

And I'd fold faster than Hamlet spotting his dad's ghost.

To study or not to study?

Let's just say, the lassi always took off before the textbook did.

Back home, Mummy was going full Ekta Kapoor mode.

Her dialogues? Emmy-worthy.

"Kahaan the itni der tak?"

"College main padhe ho ya ghumne gaye ho?"

"Tumhein padhai ki koi fikr hai bhi ya nahi?"

All delivered with the expression of a woman who had just found out her son had eloped with a syllabus he never opened.

Add to that: dramatic background score = pressure cooker whistle + TV serial violin intro.

Tears.

Moral monologues.

And at least one "Mujhe tumse yeh ummeed nahi thi."

Honestly, even Shakespeare couldn't write mothers like ours.

Lady Macbeth washed her hands obsessively.

Indian moms wash your reputation.

Papa, of course, was posted in Srinagar. The man who could've been my defender, my fellow team player, was miles away, while I fought emotional ones every evening.

So for two days after every dramatic outburst, I'd sit straight, study hard, and behave like Bharat, waiting patiently for Lord Ram to return from exile-noble, disciplined, borderline saintly.

But then… the hostel boys would show up like an uninvited baraat.

Loud, dramatic, and armed with terrible ideas.

And just like that, my vanvaas-worthy resolve would vanish faster than my pocket money in Nik Baker's.

And suddenly, I was back to gedi routes, bunks, and canteen. Because that's what friends are for-To rescue you from being too sorted.

Honestly, my life at DAV felt less like college and more like an unreleased Shakespeare play-

Much Ado About Midterms *or* A Midsummer Night's Assignment.

Full of comedy, misplaced priorities, and a plot twist every Sunday night when Mummy checked my drawer and found zero notes but a perfectly folded Domino's bill.

But through all the melodrama, masala, and the "mujhe kuch kehna hai" family scenes-

one thing remained true:

College didn't just teach me subjects.

It taught me balance.

Between friends and focus.

Between gedi routes and group studies.

Between Mummy's emotional outbursts and my own inner chaos.

You see, while I was figuring out my place in college, Mummy was juggling way more than anyone saw.

Taking care of Apoorva every single day, with patience stitched into every breath-

She didn't need a counsellor.

She needed a reason to smile.

So, I became that reason.

At least I tried to be.

Even if I couldn't take away her stress, I could make her laugh.

Pull a face. Crack a joke. Narrate my day like a one-man stand-up act.

Apoorva deserved joy, and Mummy deserved lightness.

So I kept the fun alive at home-because someone had to.

Looking back, I realize-that was my first real lesson in emotional intelligence.

Before corporate trainings and HR workshops gave it fancy names.

I learnt how to listen.

How to hold space for people.

How to balance banter with sensitivity.

And honestly?

If I had to go back, I wouldn't change a thing.

Except maybe... study a bit more before the Economics finals.

(But hey, even Adam Smith would understand.)

Chapter 7

The MBA Remix: UK Edition

"There is a tide in the affairs of men, which, taken at the flood, leads on to fortune."

– William Shakespeare

They say destiny has its own odd sense of humor. What seemed like a childhood tragedy -an abdomen injury that benched me from every game field -had unknowingly set the stage for the moment I cleared the scholarship essay with flying colors.

While the world outside played cricket matches and chased footballs, I spent years playing brain matches across chess boards, turning pages of novels thicker than my school textbooks, and learning to channel my restless energies into quiet reflection and steady reading.

When the time came for the selection, while others polished their resumes, I found myself polishing paragraphs. That essay -the one key to Birmingham -wasn't just written, it was lived, long before pen met paper.

And so, from the heart of Bangalore's lecture halls to the corridors of IBS Hyderabad -the chosen few, all bound for Birmingham, were gathered.

This was no ordinary departure. This was the quiet beginning of an extraordinary arrival.

IBS Hyderabad had become the gateway for a circle of bright-eyed aspirants -the select few who had cleared the scholarship academic gauntlet and earned their ticket to Birmingham.

It's funny how destiny knows exactly when to shuffle the deck. Scattered across different cities, we'd never crossed paths, never exchanged a word -in fact, most of us wouldn't have even recognized each other in a crowd. But one scholarship list changed all that. IBS Hyderabad became the place where strangers, stitched together by a shared dream, slowly turned into friends -the kind you carry for life.

There was an unspoken energy in the air, the kind of wide-eyed excitement that only students on the edge of their first international college adventure can truly understand. Those sunlit lawns weren't just part of the campus -they became the waiting room where our individual stories paused, only to be rewritten together.

Mornings were spent attending legal studies classes tailored for international management students, and afternoons were claimed by case study seminars -all designed not just to help us clear exams, but to sharpen the kind of thinking that could one day make us sound smarter in future boardrooms.

But the real lessons never showed up on the timetable. Over rounds of chai, coffee, and canteen Maggie, polite introductions gave way to inside jokes, and from formal hellos to personal stories. We weren't just preparing for an overseas semester; we were unknowingly assembling a crew for a journey that would outlast boarding passes and return dates.

From group currency exchange runs to mall outings, from travel checklist debates to last-minute packing disasters -the days at IBS Hyderabad stitched us together like pieces of a puzzle. Different personalities, one shared excitement.

And then came the moment that quietly made it all feel real. Not the classroom lectures, not the flight bookings, not even the visa interviews. The real shift happened the day we stepped into the currency exchange office -wide-eyed, quietly buzzing, and doing our best to look more grown-up than we felt.

The process was straightforward, but the emotions weren't. Watching familiar, slightly crumpled Indian rupee notes slide across the glass counter and return as crisp British Pounds felt like the first true confirmation that this wasn't just another college assignment. It wasn't even our own hard-earned money -but the weight of those foreign notes in our hands was enough to make the adventure feel suddenly, undeniably real.

The world beyond campus walls wasn't just a dream anymore. It was waiting.

The excitement was a living, breathing thing by now, buzzing through the hostel hallways like static before a storm.

Total, there were around 50 to 63 students selected from across all campuses -some bound for the UK, others for Australia (Adelaide). The college made sure every formality was ticked off, including our group trip to VFS Global. That day, dressed in our sharpest "interview-ready" clothes, clutching documents like golden tickets, we stood in line swapping travel plans and daydreams. The queue wasn't just a line; it was the waiting room to a brand-new Chapter.

And then came the crescendo -the airport.

Passports clutched in hand, boarding passes crisp and uncreased, parents standing close, quietly locking away emotions behind half-smiles. Friends trading last-minute advice, some serious, most half-baked, and hearts pounding against rib cages like a drum roll before the curtains rise.

Papa had come to see me off -(he had left the Army and was in Hyderabad then as the Principal of Hyderabad Public School). Watching him there, standing tall as both father and mentor, it struck me: this wasn't just another journey. This was the closing line of one Chapter, and the opening sentence of another. A quiet nod to the years of lessons, the unspoken faith that had carried me to this gate.

It was one of those moments, the kind great writers use to mark the turning points in a story. It wasn't the end of one Chapter, but the beginning of something much bigger.

The moment we boarded the plane, it felt less like an international flight and more like a college fest at 35,000 feet. The excitement was so high, I don't think anyone even registered the safety instructions -except maybe the professors, who had resigned to the chaos that was bound to unfold the minute the seatbelt signs went off.

The plane hadn't even taken off yet, and we were already busy -taking selfies, switching seats, waving at each other across the aisle like kids on a school bus. Some were busy digging into the in-flight magazines as if they'd found hidden treasure, others adjusting their headsets trying to figure out the entertainment system like it was a puzzle waiting to be solved.

When the engines finally roared to life and the plane started taxiing down the runway, a ripple of cheers and claps spread across our group, as if the plane was lifting off purely on the strength of our collective excitement. Friends were giggling non-stop, some trying to mimic the pilot's announcements in their best "British" accents, others just too busy planning all the places they'd explore once we landed.

Mid-air, the party only got better. One of the stewards must've taken a special liking to me, because he kept sneaking me double glasses of orange screwdrivers along with endless rounds of dry snacks. It felt less like air travel and more like a flying lounge.

The more the drinks kept coming, the more the volume rose -card games were pulled out, playlists were shared, and seats were swapped faster than the seatbelt signs could light up. The rest of the passengers? Well, let's just say the faces around us ranged from mildly annoyed to fully horrified, as the loud, happy Indian bunch turned the plane into a mid-air college dorm.

But in that moment, none of us cared. We were flying abroad for the first time. The sky belonged to us, and the world was waiting.

With a brief stop at Doha, Qatar, the city unfolded beneath us like a well-planned maze of modernity -clean lines, neat streets, and that unmistakable golden desert glow stretching to the horizon. But after a short layover, it was time to board the flight to London.

The excitement was almost electric. It wasn't just the thrill of flying, or the novelty of being thousands of feet above the clouds -it was the quiet realization that all those months of planning, packing, and daydreaming had finally led us here.

After all, we weren't just traveling; we were on the verge of a life-changing adventure. Most of us were still grinning ear to ear, unable to shake off the excitement of flying abroad for the first time.

When we finally landed in London, the Queen didn't roll out the red carpet, but the airport did offer the next best thing -free Lyca Mobile SIM cards, stacked on racks like apples in Eden, waiting for a bunch of wide-eyed, jet-lagged students to commit the original sin of greed. And commit we did. True to the timeless Indian instinct -why take one when you can take five? -we pocketed them with the grace of seasoned opportunists.

Once our loot was secured, we wheeled our luggage out to the black coaches parked like sentries at the curb. The bus driver, as stern as a Head Master on inspection day, barked out the same warning on loop: "Seatbelts, please." Buckling up on a moving bus wasn't exactly the rebellion-worthy hill we wanted to die on, so we clicked in, though our minds were far too busy drinking in the foreign skyline to bother with earthly rules.

The road from London to Birmingham stretched out for about two and a half hours -though you'd never guess it by the look on our faces. Jet lag? Fatigue? Mere mortals might've felt it, but not us. Our excitement had the stamina of a Shakespearean soliloquy: dramatic, unending, and utterly immune to the ticking clock.

By the time the city lights of Birmingham blinked into view, the sky was already clocking out for the day, but our enthusiasm was still working overtime. At the hotel, the professors handed out room keys and breakfast coupons, which -in that moment -felt less like scraps of paper and more like winning lottery tickets.

Our temporary palace sat perfectly poised between the University of Birmingham and Austin Uni -or as the locals call it, 'Uni.' Yes, apparently in this brave new world, syllables were an endangered species, and the word 'University' had fallen victim first.

I was rooming with Amarjot -a fine companion for the grand art of lying awake and marveling at life's absurdities.

That night, sleep stood no chance. We sat there, wide-eyed, half in disbelief, half in delight, chewing over the simple fact that we were in a brand new city, halfway across the world. The kind of moment that makes you wonder whether life's been generous or just plain sneaky.

Morning came with its own little rituals -a hotel breakfast that tasted better simply because it was stamped "abroad," and the customary photo ops that future nostalgia would no doubt be grateful for.

The campus sat just a casual ten-minute stroll away, but our pace wasn't built for speed. It was the kind of walk where the air hums with possibility, and your feet barely touch the ground.

After a quick round of photo ops -the type our future selves would thank us for -we joined the rest of the crew for the short ten-minute stroll to campus.

As expected, most of us from Hyderabad stuck together like overcooked rice -old friendships make the best compass when everything else feels new. And standing there with familiar faces, on unfamiliar streets, I realized this wasn't just another day of classes. This was the start of a story we'd talk about for years.

On day one, in a stroke of professorial wisdom (or perhaps to ensure none of us would get lost and spark an international incident), our shepherds -I mean, professors -marched us off for a walking tour of the neighborhood. Fate, ever the playwright, seemed in an especially dramatic mood. Just as we rounded a corner, there stood none other than Anil Kapoor himself, mid-shoot, eyebrows arched and charm levels set to maximum.

Talk about a cinematic welcome -our first day abroad, and Bollywood had already found us. Somewhere, the universe was winking.

Once the starstruck fog lifted and our stomachs resumed their protest, we wandered into the nearest McDonald's, expecting familiar comfort. Ah, but the plot thickened! The vegetarian options were as scarce as honest politicians, and in the great spirit of blind trust, a few comrades bit into their burgers -only to discover, post-bite, that they'd just inducted themselves into the Beef Appreciation Society.

Let's just say... some faces turned shades of regret Shakespeare himself never thought to pen.

Me? I stuck to a humble baguette -a reliable 99 pence investment that neither betrayed my palate nor offended my conscience. A modest choice, but in foreign lands, safety is a virtue, and sandwiches don't lie.

The days that followed settled into a rhythm only students abroad would understand -a fine blend of pseudo-adulthood and full-throttle freeloading. Breakfast was covered, thanks to those golden coupons that felt more like Willy Wonka's tickets to survival than mere meal vouchers.

But lunch and dinner? Ah, now that was a game of wits, hunger, and the delicate art of stretching a pound until it squealed. I, ever the prudent economist (and part-time cheapskate), discovered that a humble baguette from the corner store could outlast both appetite and ambition -all for 99 pence. Buttered, toasted, or simply devoured in its plain, crusty glory, it became my loyal companion through many a cash-strapped evening.

For the homesick and the spice-starved, there was Kohinoor -a Bangladeshi-run joint that served Indian dishes with enough masala to cure heartache and homesickness in one go. What started as the occasional rescue mission for our desi taste buds quickly evolved into a full-fledged tiffin arrangement. Orders were shared, biryanis debated, naans negotiated, and for a brief, turmeric-scented moment -the Midlands almost felt like home.

And for the brave or the broke (usually both), Tesco's ready-to-eat aisle stood like a lighthouse for lost souls. There's no bonding experience quite like microwaving a dubious-looking curry at 1 am while your roommate questions every life choice that led you to this fine dining moment.

Of course, birthdays abroad hit a little differently. Mine conveniently landed on a weekend, which meant no classes, no deadlines -just the open road and a rickety train bound for Warwick. The castle stood there in all its medieval might, draped in that permanent English fog that makes everything look straight out of a Sherlock Holmes novel.

The moment we stepped off the train, it felt like we'd walked straight onto the pages of a fairytale, minus the dragons and plus a lot more pigeons. Warwick Castle stood tall and brooding, its stone walls probably still echoing the swords and scandals of centuries past. We wandered through its winding paths, pausing to click photos and pretend we were lost members of British royalty. (Spoiler: the accent didn't stick, but the excitement sure did.)

The nearby university grounds looked like something out of a postcard, and the surrounding houses were so quaint, I half expected a hobbit to swing open a door and invite us in for tea. It was the kind of place where every brick whispered stories, and every chimney seemed to puff with quiet pride.

But the birthday tour didn't stop there. Once the travel bug bit, we were giddy with wanderlust. The holidays became our golden ticket to backpack across the UK, trading comfort for adventure. Cardiff was our first pit stop, with its rain-soaked streets and Welsh charm -the kind of place where your shoes are never dry, and the locals have the warmest smiles, probably because they've made peace with the weather.

Then came Glasgow, where we sipped tea at the People's Palace, trying to act all intellectual and grown-up, while secretly planning our next round of mischief. Edinburgh, though, was the crown jewel -a city so beautiful it could make even the grumpiest traveler wax poetic. Gothic spires, winding alleys, castles perched dramatically on hills -every corner felt like the opening scene of an Oscar-winning period drama. (Papa had told me to visit it as his English teacher from his school days, who had gone on a scholarship there, had spun quite a few yarns about this charming city and its majestic castle).

And then there were the Highlands. Ah, the Highlands! Where the snow lies in wait, ready to humble every city kid who thought suede leather shoes were a brilliant idea for winter trekking. One moment I was frolicking like some amateur adventurer; the next, I was ankle-deep in snow, shoes drenched, dignity frozen, and nose running faster than my legs could keep up.

To top it off, as we journeyed back to Birmingham, the weather turned hostile. Blizzard winds slapped us around like unpaid extras in a disaster movie, temperatures plunged to a cheerful minus 18 degrees, and I learned that hypothermia wasn't just a Chapter in our school science books.

But here's the funny thing about youth -the cold might freeze your fingers, but it can't chill your spirit. By the time we got back, half-frozen but still wide-eyed, we were already plotting the next escape.

No international program is ever complete without the sacred ritual known as the "industrial visit" -that fine educational tradition where universities dress up field trips in formal shoes and PowerPoint presentations, and hope you'll emerge more employable by the end of the bus ride.

Our first stop was the Jaguar Land Rover plant -a place so pristine and polished, I felt underdressed just standing in the lobby. The machines moved with such precision that even the robots seemed to have better work ethics than most humans I knew. The tour guide, with the enthusiasm of a man who'd seen one too many wide-eyed students before us, rattled off facts about engine assembly lines and vehicle testing while we nodded thoughtfully, trying hard to look like future CEOs or at least tried to- while secretly wondering if the vending machine near the exit accepted coins or card.

As I stood there, watching machines and men move in perfect harmony -every bolt tightened, every part slotted in without a hiccup -I couldn't help but wonder if this was what adulthood was meant to look like. A world where everything runs on time, systems click into place, and outcomes are as predictable as a German engineer's coffee break. But standing there, I knew my own life was anything but a precision-built engine. If anything, it felt more like a battered bike, coughing its way through Bangalore traffic -stalled, overheated, and occasionally pushed by sheer hope and a bit of luck. Still, a man can aspire. After all, isn't growth just the art of learning to tighten your own loose bolts, one roadside breakdown at a time?

Then came Cadbury World -though calling it an "industrial visit" felt like an insult to both industry and imagination. It was less of a factory tour and more of a carefully orchestrated pilgrimage, designed to turn grown men into wide-eyed children before they'd even stepped past the gift shop.

The moment the doors opened, the scent of molten cocoa wrapped itself around us like an old childhood blanket -soft, warm, and utterly disarming. I've always believed the folks at Cadbury are less confectioners and more sorcerers; no mortal scent should have the power to dissolve the weight of youthful skepticism in under thirty seconds. One deep breath, and your brain would promptly abandon any pretense of MBA-level curiosity, replacing it with a single, unwavering mantra: Chocolate first, questions later.

We wandered through the maze of glass partitions, watching with the reverence of temple-goers as conveyor belts carried half-formed chocolates to their destiny. The machines worked with clinical, clockwork precision, churning out perfect Dairy Milk bars at a pace that would leave even the most efficient factory workers in awe. Somewhere between the shiny stainless steel tanks and robotic arms, I felt a quiet truth sneak up on me -the comforting notion I'd carried as a child, that chocolates were probably handmade by a brigade of plump grandmothers in hairnets, had been crushed under the sheer weight of modern manufacturing.

And yet, I wasn't bitter. Not one bit. The free samples had seen to that. You see, some truths in life are easier to swallow when they're wrapped in smooth milk chocolate.

We were even shown the so-called "delicate art" of chocolate-making -which, as it turns out, mostly involved watching machines do all the heavy lifting, while we stood there, noses pressed to the glass, mentally calculating the odds of vaulting over the barrier and diving headfirst into a vat of liquid Dairy Milk.

The highlight, of course, wasn't the engineering marvels or the corporate history lessons -it was the shameless, sugar-laden spree of samples, which I consumed under the noble guise of 'research.' Some lessons, I learned, are best digested one bite at a time.

Our scholarly pilgrimage wasn't destined to be limited to the four walls of a lecture hall in Birmingham. Oh no, the professors, in their infinite wisdom (or perhaps in an attempt to tire us into submission), had other plans. They packed us into coaches and sent us rolling through the English countryside, bound for places that lived in history books long before they ever made it onto Google Maps.

First on the map: Oxford -a place so soaked in prestige that even the pigeons seemed to strut around with honorary degrees. As we strolled past those ancient, ivy-clad colleges, I couldn't help but feel like I'd stepped onto the set of some grand period drama. The air itself felt different -crisper, heavier, as though it was carrying the collective weight of centuries of intellectual struggle and too many cups of tea. The lecture we attended inside one of those hallowed halls felt like the sort of thing that would make your parents believe every penny spent on your education was finally justified. I didn't understand half of it, but I did leave with a new appreciation for the art of nodding thoughtfully while your brain quietly takes a nap.

And then there was Stratford-upon-Avon -the birthplace of the man whose words have tortured generations of schoolchildren and delighted just as many theatre-goers: Mr. William Shakespeare himself. Walking along the streets there felt like time travel, the kind where you half expect to bump into the Bard, quill in hand, scribbling away his next tragedy while sipping a pint. The houses leaned into the street as if they, too, were eavesdropping on the tourists. The whole place was equal parts charming and humbling -a gentle reminder that great legacies can spring from the most unassuming little towns.

A few days later, our ever-determined professors -convinced that true global exposure couldn't be confined to PowerPoint slides and pre-reads -packed us onto yet another coach and pointed us toward London. The city where centuries of monarchy, markets, and masterful branding have coexisted so effortlessly that even their pigeons seem to have an upper-class accent.

Once there, the academic itinerary was swiftly reduced to a thin sheet of suggestions, the kind that gave you just enough structure to call it "curriculum" but enough loopholes to call it "freedom." In true MBA fashion, we optimized our resources -which is to say, we ditched the plan and went for maximum 'experiential learning' on foot.

From the towering formality of Big Ben to the unapologetic self-advertisement of the London Eye, every landmark offered its own crash course in either marketing, real estate, or customer psychology. Buckingham Palace? The longest-standing case study in personal branding. Oxford Street? A masterclass in consumer behavior. The Tube? Well, that taught us the value of time management, spatial awareness, and the British art of quietly resenting strangers without making eye contact.

By the time evening rolled in, the city's real MBA module began: Networking 101, Pub Edition.

The British, I realized, don't simply clock out -they flow, pint in hand, straight from spreadsheets to stouts. And as MBA students armed with student discount cards (God's gift to broke future executives), we took full advantage of the local economy. Consider it fieldwork. Market research, if you will, into human behavior after two drinks.

Every corner of London seemed to whisper the same unspoken business lesson:

"It's not about the grades you earn, but the stories you collect."

Back in Birmingham, life quickly settled into a rhythm that felt suspiciously close to adulthood -the kind where you juggle lectures, laundry, self-doubt, and the occasional burst of misplaced confidence, all before your morning coffee.

Mornings were reserved for runs -or, in my case, noble attempts at convincing myself that I was a "runner." Birmingham, with its charming mix of old-world bricks and modern glass, unfolded like a living postcard on those crisp, quiet mornings. Somewhere between pretending I was training for a marathon and actually catching my breath, I stumbled upon two discoveries that would shape my stay:

One, the local Gurudwara, standing calm and grounded amid the city's concrete hustle. It wasn't long before a small bunch of us -fellow students running equally low on homesickness immunity -started showing up, rolling up our sleeves, and doing seva. There was something quietly profound about washing dishes in an unfamiliar land, shoulder-to-shoulder with strangers who felt like family by the second chapati. The kind of lesson no MBA textbook would ever teach: humility doesn't show up on your résumé, but it shapes your character better than any leadership seminar.

Two, the holy grail of budget grooming: a no-frills barber shop in one of the city's tucked-away lanes, run by a cheerful crew of African barbers. Their business model was elegantly simple: £5, no scissors, only trimmers -"same price whether you lose one inch or one identity crisis." In an economy where a decent haircut could cost as much as a week's groceries, this was entrepreneurship at its finest.

Evenings, though, were when the city truly came alive. Birmingham had the sort of nightlife that could teach even the driest of MBA case studies a thing or two about customer retention. The pubs weren't just watering holes -they were boardrooms without PowerPoint, where strangers sealed lifelong bonds over discounted pitchers and pub quizzes, often forgetting names but remembering stories.

And so, between classroom lectures on Marketing Management -where professors dissected brand strategies with all the seriousness of world leaders signing peace treaties -and our own off-the-record "field research" at the local pubs, I stumbled upon a quiet, unspoken truth.

It didn't matter how sleek the design, how flashy the pitch, or how complicated the jargon -whether it was a product, a business, or even a person -at the end of the day, it was the story that sold.

The narrative. The emotion. The connection.

And if you ever wanted a crash course in that, all you had to do was watch a group of students from different corners of the world, armed with nothing but a student discount card and a mild thirst for adventure, turning clinking pint glasses into cultural bridges.

Now, don't mistake me for a drinker. I've never been the "cheers to the weekend" sort. But when you're surrounded by friends, sharing laughter and swapping stories across sticky wooden tables, sometimes even a sip of beer feels less like drinking and more like soaking in the moment.

And if you ask me, that's marketing too -the subtle art of making even a non-drinker raise a glass, just to toast the memory.

Classroom life at Birmingham was, in its own way, a rather humbling theatre of reality checks. Back at IBS Hyderabad, we had all mastered the sacred art of "Ctrl+C, Ctrl+V" -the great academic shortcut that had carried many students through dire nights and deadlined mornings.

But Birmingham? Oh no, this was a different battlefield altogether.

One fine afternoon, the university unveiled its most feared invention: the Plagiarism Report -a cold, merciless document that listed names and their matching percentage scores with the precision of a guillotine. Imagine my face when I discovered I'd topped the list -and not in the proud, scholarship-worthy way.

In that single moment, I realized that adulthood -much like assignments in the UK -offered no shortcuts. No copy-paste. No last-minute rescues. You either showed up with your own work, or you got schooled -quite literally.

So I did what any self-respecting MBA student would do after an academic scandal: I mended my ways. I learned the fine art of referencing, the noble struggle of paraphrasing, and the quiet dignity of typing every painful word by hand, like a modern-day Shakespeare facing his first term paper.

In the midst of this academic awakening, life had other lessons lined up. Manorath Joshi -one of my close friends -was struggling with a stubborn back injury that grew worse by the day. I'd help him as much as I could:

from rubbing ointments onto his back to lending him moral support when the pain became unbearable.

Eventually, when even his resilience tapped out, Manorath made the tough call to head home to Mumbai. I traveled with him to London to see him off -a bittersweet journey, where friendship and farewell rode side by side, as if teaching me the MBA of life: sometimes, the strongest bonds aren't measured in shared notes, but in quiet acts of care.

Looking back, that plagiarism list was less of an academic hiccup and more of a personal plot twist. Funny how it takes a scarlet letter on a university notice board to remind you that some lessons aren't about books, grades, or clever shortcuts -they're about growing up.

For the first time, it hit me that hard work wasn't just a motivational poster cliché. There was no charm, no jugaad, no last-minute rescue team in this new world. Here, the only thing standing between you and success was the effort you were willing to put in -word by honest word, hour by sleepless hour.

I started approaching assignments the way life demands. We approach everything worth having -with patience, commitment, and the understanding that shortcuts might save time, but they steal the journey.

It wasn't about the grades anymore; it was about earning the quiet, personal pride of knowing that the work was mine, start to finish. In a way, Birmingham taught me more about integrity than any classroom ever could.

Adulthood, I was beginning to understand, is less about freedom and more about the discipline to handle that freedom well. *And perhaps that's the first real MBA lesson: life doesn't reward the fastest hands or the smoothest talkers -it rewards the ones who show up, do the work, and stay the course.*

That incident wasn't just a wake-up call in academics; it was a turning point in my life. It marked the birth of Aman 3.0, an upgraded version of myself. After the surgery that had forced Aman 2.0 to slow down, I began to truly rethink things. Gone were the days of shortcuts and quick fixes. I came to realize that, like any product, the true value doesn't lie in its flashy appearance or easy solutions -it's in the story it tells. And in that moment, I understood something crucial: real success is earned, not borrowed. The lesson was clear -hard work and originality are the only currencies that truly matter, both in class and in life. I could no longer take the easy route; I had to build my own story, one step at a time, and earn my place the honest way.

Ah, the London trip with Manorath -that's when things started to feel like a proper adventure. Manorath and I had become pretty close friends, and, as life would have it, we found ourselves in London together, navigating the city with all the enthusiasm of two kids on a treasure hunt. The trip wasn't just about sightseeing; it was a test of how far you could stretch your curiosity, like a rubber band ready to snap at any moment. Our first stop? Imperial College -one of those places you only hear about in awe-filled whispers back in India. And let me tell you, it lived up to the hype. I'd always been a bit skeptical about "prestige" before, but stepping into that place felt like being handed a key to a whole new world. We met a few students from there, and, truth be told, I couldn't help but wonder if I was seeing the future of academia -or at least the future of student loans.

After the meetups at Imperial, we took a detour to the famous Chelsea Football Stadium. Now, I don't claim to be a die-hard football fan, but standing there, surrounded by the history of the game, I could almost hear the chants of the crowd. It was like the air itself had been infused with the passion of every match that had ever been played there. I found myself getting swept up in the moment, imagining the players charging down the field. Manorath, of course, was practically giddy. He had the kind of energy that made you feel like you were witnessing greatness, even if you didn't know the offside rule from football.

The real cherry on top, though, came with Boxing Day, when the city seemed to slow down in the most magical way possible. With all the post-Christmas sales in full swing, it felt like the universe was handing out discounts on life. Manorath and I went on our own little shopping spree, snatching up perfumes, gifts for home, and whatever else caught our eye. The discounts were so ridiculous, I half-expected the store owners to start thanking us for taking their stock off their hands. It wasn't just about buying stuff, though; it was about being in a place where everyone was caught up in the afterglow of the holidays, just a little bit lighter, a little bit freer.

Between football stadiums, university meetups, and wandering around like two kids with too much energy and not enough time, London became more than just a city -it became an experience. And honestly, by the time we hopped on a flight back to India, I had a suitcase full of souvenirs, memories, and a renewed sense of what it meant to take life as it came, with a little curiosity, a little adventure, and a whole lot of humor.

While Birmingham had done its fair share of reshaping me, it was the people outside the classroom who added the finishing touches. Somewhere between assignments and weekend explorations, I had stitched together a patchwork of friendships with strangers -folks from Manchester, Poland, Pakistan, and corners of the world I'd only ever spotted on a map during Geography classes. It's funny how, in a foreign land, the walls you carry around back home seem to fall away. Conversations with these new faces weren't forced or filtered; they were genuine -the kind of easy, unhurried chats that made you forget nationalities, time zones, and even your own limited worldviews.

One of those unlikely friendships was with a taxi driver -the kind of man who, in another life, would've made an excellent philosopher, if only the world had bothered to listen. He wasn't just our driver, he was our unofficial tour guide, history professor, and sometimes, even a silent therapist as we rode out of the city in search of the next postcard-worthy memory.

One of those rides took us to Liverpool -a place that, much like life itself, taught me that icons aren't born in glass towers or spotless boardrooms, but in small, unassuming cities. Standing there, amidst the birthplace of The Beatles, the grand architecture, and the electric pulse of football fandom, I could almost feel history brush past me. It was the kind of place that reminded you -greatness isn't always loud; sometimes, it's quietly carved into old bricks, waiting for curious eyes to notice.

And then, like all good things, the UK Chapter drew to a close. We flew out from Heathrow, this time with hearts heavier than our luggage. There was a layover in Dubai, but the real pause was within me. Somewhere between the takeoffs and landings, I realized I wasn't the same Aman who had first set foot on British soil months ago. The boy who had arrived, armed with overconfidence and half-baked plans, was quietly replaced by someone else. Someone a little more thoughtful. A little more aware of the world's infinite possibilities -and his own limitations.

By the time we finally touched down in Hyderabad, it wasn't just my passport that had collected stamps. My mind had, too. New lessons, new friendships, new failures, new flavors of humility. I'd boarded the plane as a student chasing an MBA degree, but I stepped off it as a young man who now understood -education isn't confined to classrooms, and life doesn't hand out certificates, only experiences.

The air felt different, even though the humidity was the same. The streets looked the same, but my eyes had learnt to notice more than just traffic signals and U-turns. And my old room? It had waited patiently, like a loyal retriever, still the same, but greeting a new version of its owner.

You see, some journeys don't announce their transformations with medals or certificates. Sometimes, the biggest upgrade slips in quietly, like software updating overnight -and you only notice the difference when life throws you the next challenge and you find yourself... ready.

I didn't return as the boy who had left. I returned as someone better. Not perfect, but better. More evolved, more patient, a little more curious about people, and just a tad more forgiving -both toward others and myself.

Chapter 8

"Monday to Monday:
The Corporate Loop"

I wasn't born for consultant solution sales. Let's clear that up right away. I was meant for a much simpler existence -preferably as a part-time philosopher, full-time chai drinker, sitting on a breezy hilltop in Mussoorie, staring thoughtfully into the distance and occasionally pretending to write.

But life, with its world-class sense of humor (and a knack for timing), had other plans. It took one long, thoughtful look at me -a fellow blessed with what my mother proudly (and, let's be honest, a touch too enthusiastically) referred to as "very good looks" -and probably thought, "Alright, let's not get carried away here. It's not the face that's going to close deals."

Turns out, it wasn't the looks or the so-called charm that was going to seal the deal. What really did the trick was a smooth tongue, honed over years of school debates, recitations, and, of course, mandatory indoor diplomacy (thanks to an abdomen injury that swapped my childhood football dreams for marathon conversations). Throw in a dangerously high level of empathy -the kind that could negotiate peace treaties if needed -and the universe figured- "Sales, my friend. Solution sales. That's where your charm and childhood injuries will finally pay rent."

Of course, "solutions" made perfect sense. I was already solving virtual world problems on my PlayStation -corporate boardrooms couldn't be that different.

And here we are.

Now before you assume I'm the next Wolf of Wall Street, let me assure you: I don't name the companies I've worked for, not because I'm shy, but because if I did, they might send me an invoice asking for commission on this book. Let's just say I joined a solutions-sales team. A good one. A very good one, in fact. The kind that makes your relatives raise their eyebrows at family dinners and say, "Oh, beta, that's impressive."

There's a rhythm to sales, a kind of invisible symphony where the instruments are your words, your expressions, and your ability to listen more than you speak (contrary to popular belief, sales isn't about yapping until the customer faints). The process is simple -well, deceptively simple:

Catch my vibe. Follow my pitch. Fall for my charm. Sign the deal.

That's the order of operations. Notice "Buy my product" comes last. First, you sell yourself, your intent, your understanding, your handshake, your coffee order. The product just tags along for the ride.

I quickly learned sales isn't about trickery or manipulation. It's about empathy. It's about stepping into the customer's worn-out shoes and walking around long enough to understand where they pinch. It's about solving a problem, not shoving a product. Think less

Shakespeare's "All the world's a stage" and more Mark Twain's "If you tell the truth, you don't have to remember anything." Because in sales, if you're faking it -trust me, the customer will smell it even before you've finished your elevator pitch.

And yes, I know what you're thinking. "You must be one of those ATANA types -All Talk And No Action." I'm flattered you think I talk so well, but no. If I didn't back my words with action, no company would have paid my bills, forget promoting me. Somewhere along the way, I learnt that sales is actually more about CRM than charm. Customer Relationship Management, for the uninitiated-though, funnily enough, both require the same core ingredient: being human.

Selling, contrary to the horror stories, isn't about being pushy. It's a knowledge-intensive, empathy-led process. You learn to read the room, read the customer, and, sometimes, read the company's unspoken budget limits like an underpaid Sherlock Holmes.

So, while I wasn't designed for sales, I think I grew into it rather well. Or, as I like to believe, sales grew into me. Either way, the bills are paid, the customers are happy, and my coffee addiction stays funded.

Now, let's talk about Solution Sales. And no, it's not just a fancy term for "selling stuff." It's about providing solutions, my friend. You know, solving problems like a well-timed plot twist in a mystery novel. It's like when you've been stuck on a level in your favorite PlayStation game for hours, your patience wearing thin, and then-BOOM-you figure out the perfect move that saves the day. That moment when everything clicks and you realize, "Ah, this is how it's done." That's Solution Sales. Only, instead of a controller, you're wielding knowledge, empathy, and, of course, a little bit of charm.

Now, I know what you're thinking: "This guy's a sales guy, right? He must be all about flashy pitches and closing deals." Well, not exactly. I wasn't born wired for selling -my childhood sales pitch rarely made it past "Mummy, can I have one more chocolate?" I was more into late-night binge-watching cartoons and reading Asterix and Obelix-stuff that doesn't exactly scream 'business tycoon.' But somehow, life threw me into this arena. It's not about pushing products; it's about providing answers to problems no one even knew they had. It's like that feeling when you finally beat a level you've been stuck on for days-sweet, rewarding, and totally worth it.

So, how does one go from gaming to consulting? Simple: the skills are oddly transferable. Think about it: in video games, you analyze the situation, identify the problem, and then, through sheer strategy, solve it. In Solution Sales, it's the same thing. You identify the client's pain points (I'll spare you the metaphor of slaying dragons), you map out the solution, and then you deliver the fix. It's not about pitching a product; it's about presenting a well-thought-out strategy that makes the client think, "Wow, this is exactly what we need."

And yes, just like in Asterix, where the team has to outsmart the Romans with clever tricks and solutions, you've got to use your wits, not just your pitch. It's about understanding the client's world, navigating the intricacies of their needs, and then-here's the magic part-making them believe that the solution you've crafted is their own idea. You know, just like that one moment in every cartoon where the hero suddenly gets it and says, "I've got an idea!"-and bam, the solution falls right into place.

The best part? Watching the client's eyes light up when you deliver that perfect solution. It's like finishing a game level you've been grinding through for hours. The victory is sweet, but it's even sweeter when you know you've solved something that truly matters.

So, while I may have started out as a kid navigating the world of video games, cartoons, and Asterix books, I've somehow found myself solving real-world problems-and, spoiler alert-actually enjoying it. Who knew, right?

If childhood had offered a crystal ball, I doubt "solution sales" would've flashed on the screen. Back then, my "solutions" involved figuring out how to pause the PlayStation right before Mummy walked in, or negotiating extended cartoon marathons when homework was breathing down my neck. Asterix comics sharpened my strategy; video games taught me resource management; and trying to outwit my parents built my negotiation skills.

Turns out, all that "wasted time" was just an early internship for corporate life. Who knew?

Because real-world sales -or should I say, solution consulting -isn't about dumping products on the next poor soul who picks up your call. It's about knowing when to speak, when to pause, and when to let silence close the deal. It's about empathy, curiosity, and the fine art of not pushing, but guiding. A lot like convincing your dad that your new phone isn't a luxury, but a necessity for "school research."

Some people think sales is about glib talk. Truth is, it's about solving puzzles. Human puzzles. Business puzzles. Cultural puzzles. You walk into a client's office (or log into yet another painfully polite Teams call) and start decoding:

What's their real problem?

What are they trying to fix, avoid, or quietly ignore?

Where do I fit in?

And when you finally crack the code -offer the right solution, not the flashiest product -you watch the magic unfold. That's the thrill. That's the real game.

But no cheat codes here -just patience, practice, and enough coffee to fuel a small army.

The way I see it, I'm not here to close a deal -I'm here to build a place in the customer's story, one that lasts for many Chapters. I'm an actor, stepping onto a stage.

The script? Always changing. The audience? Always skeptical. The costume? Non-negotiable.

Long before corporate boardrooms, I had mastered this craft on a far humbler stage -the living room floor. Armed with nothing but a towel-cape, I'd transform from a superhero one hour to a cartoon villain the next, switching accents, expressions, and arguments with the ease of a veteran.

Not much has changed, really. I still study my audience, learn the plot, memorize the cues, and dress the part. The stakes are just higher now -and sadly, no commercial breaks.

You see, great sales isn't about wearing the most expensive suit or speaking the loudest in the room. It's about knowing your audience so well that you become one of them. If my customers are sharp dressers, I match their sharpness. If they prefer simplicity, I fold away the flash. It's theatre, but with real consequences.

I've learned over the years -much like I learned from studying Asterix's clever plots or memorizing cartoon dialogues -that success comes not from forcing your story, but from fitting perfectly into theirs.

When you meet a customer, you don't sell. You perform. And if your performance feels authentic, if you've done your homework right, the applause isn't far behind -the deal gets signed, the company's happy, you're happy, and (let's be honest) your inbox starts filling up with incentive mails faster than you can say 'target achieved.

So yes, maybe I wasn't born for the sales life, but I was born to play parts. And life -with its perfect irony -made sure I turned that into a career.

Chapter 9

"The Corporate Balancing Act"

Ah, the glamorous world of corporate sales -where targets are as high as Mount Everest, and your coffee intake rivals that of a New York stockbroker on a Monday morning. The moment you hit your target, they move the post. It's the grown-up version of those childhood video games I loved, only this time, the reward isn't unlocking a new level but unlocking the ability to pay your EMIs.

There was a time I thought deadlines were named so because they were meant to kill you -and honestly, I wasn't too far off. Sleepless nights, back-to-back client calls, and those monthly reviews that felt more like trial hearings than meetings. The stress? Oh, it had all the qualities of an uninvited house guest -stubborn, clingy, and always showing up at the worst times.

Personal life? That poor fellow packed his bags and left a long time ago.

Hobbies? Those became legends -things I once read about in history books.

Weekends blurred into weekdays, and holidays were mere entries on the HR portal, gathering dust like unread terms and conditions.

If corporate life had a handbook, the first rule would read something like this:

"Welcome aboard. Here's your laptop, your login, and a lifetime supply of targets you'll never quite reach."

And so began my slow but steady transformation from a bright-eyed recruit into a seasoned tightrope walker -balancing targets on one shoulder, personal sanity on the other, and somehow managing not to fall flat on my face.

You see, the thing about corporate life is that it doesn't send you an invitation to a well-balanced existence. No, it shoves you headfirst into client calls, back-to-back review meetings, and Excel sheets that seem to multiply like Gremlins in a rainstorm. The hours blur, the coffee runs cold, and your hobbies slowly start filing for a missing person's report.

At one point, I even forgot that I owned a pair of running shoes. My bookshelf sat there, gathering dust, silently judging me for abandoning Asterix and Calvin & Hobbes for quarterly reports and sales decks.

But the human heart is a resilient little machine, isn't it? Mine, thankfully, had enough common sense left to raise the alarm. And so began my conscious quest for balance. A little self-rescue operation, if you will.

Somewhere between all the quarterly chaos and the never-ending pursuit of numbers, I realized I needed to claim back my little pockets of peace. The world wouldn't stop for me, so I had to slow myself down.

I began with music -trading my adrenaline-fueled playlists for soothing ragas. The change was almost magical, like swapping Red Bull for chamomile tea.

I traded late-night binge-watching for the calming company of Hindustani ragas.

I laced up my running shoes next. What began as a casual jog around the block slowly stretched into long, quiet weekend runs -sometimes 20, even 25 kilometers at a time. The same streets that once rushed past my car window now stood still, becoming my silent companions. There's a kind of clarity that only open roads and steady footsteps can offer -the kind no meeting room or PowerPoint ever could.

Running became more than just exercise; it became my anchor. It channelled my restless energy, melted away stress, and gave me space to simply... be. And on the days I wasn't running, you'd probably find me cycling. That old childhood love for two wheels never really left me; if anything, it only grew stronger. Some weekends, I'd clock close to 90 or 100 kilometers, lost in the rhythm of the pedals and the simplicity of the ride.

Meditation found its way into my mornings too, quietly helping me clear the mental clutter before the world could pile more on. One small change led to another, out went the vending machine snacks, and in came home-cooked meals even my doctor would nod at.

Slowly, the rush of life softened into rhythm. The chaos didn't disappear, but it began to sound a little less like static, and a little more like jazz.

And then there's writing. Long before this book, it was my diary that held my stories, a quiet space where scattered thoughts found a home. It's funny, flipping through old pages is what helped me piece together this one. Who knows, maybe those scribbles will lead me to the next book too.

Funny how life writes its best Chapters when you're too busy living them, and sometimes, all it takes is a pair of running shoes, a bicycle, a quiet mind, and a pen to find your way back to yourself.

Of course, no self-rescue mission is complete without calling in backup. Mine came wrapped in the most ordinary, yet most extraordinary people-family.

First rule of surviving the corporate jungle?

Call your mother. Every day. Without fail.

It's funny -no matter how many zeros your quarterly target has or how many fire-fighting emails your inbox coughs up, one call from Mummy has the magical ability to hit the reset button on your soul. Her voice has this rare quality: it can simultaneously scold you for not eating properly and remind you that the world isn't such a bad place after all.

And then there's Papa. Our weekend catch-ups usually start with a movie recommendation, drift into music trivia, and somewhere between the old classics -his favorites, which quietly became mine too: Jim Reeves, Perry Como, The Carpenters -and a debate over who played the better James Bond, I remember to breathe.

And then there's Apoorva. Our conversations don't follow rules or routines -they flow as effortlessly as only a bond written by love can. Living with cerebral palsy, she has taught me more about grace, resilience, and unconditional love than any boardroom or bestseller ever could. I am her whole world -and she, without question, is mine. In her presence, the noise of life fades. Time slows, hearts speak, and I'm reminded that the truest measure of a life well-lived isn't success or applause -it's the way you make someone feel safe, seen, and loved. Her love asks for nothing, yet it gives me everything. And all I ever want is to make sure she feels cherished, protected, and never for a moment alone in this world.

I make sure I keep my old connections alive -nurturing them like precious plants in the garden of life. Parth, my friend, my brother, is a gift that life has blessed me with. We're not just friends; we're soul brothers. Funny, considering we only met 4 or 5 years ago, but when you click like we did, it feels like we've known each other for ages. The kind of bond where even silence is comfortable, and the inside jokes pile up faster than the coffee cups. I'm always in touch with Auntie too, who's been a constant source of love and wisdom. In many ways, we're a family, not just by blood, but by heart.

Then there's Param -another friend, another brother. We make it a point to catch up whenever we can, even if life tries to pull us in opposite directions. Sometimes, it's the simplest meet-ups that remind you of what really matters. You know, the kind where we pick up right where we left off, like no time's passed, and the world outside doesn't exist for a while.

Friends like these, they keep you grounded -or, let's be honest, sometimes they force you to be grounded, whether you want to or not. They remind you that no matter how high you climb, you're never too big to share a laugh, a rant, or a ridiculously unplanned weekend getaway. They keep the chaos of life at bay -and let's face it, they're the only ones who'll still laugh at your terrible jokes when the world seems to have forgotten how.

And every week, without negotiation, I visit the temple. Not to beg for promotions or to bargain for easy clients -just to say thank you. To the universe, to the almighty, to life. Gratitude is the oldest, most reliable mental health hack.

They say weekdays build your future, but I've learned it's the weekends that shape your sanity. Those two quiet bookmarks at the end of the week hold more power than any performance review or Monday morning plan.

It's during those slower hours -when the world stops demanding and starts breathing, that I find the space to declutter my thoughts, to realign the compass, and remind myself of who I am beneath the layers of targets, emails, and half-drunk coffees.

Weekends aren't just for catching your breath; they're for rearranging your inner world. For checking in with the version of yourself that too often gets lost between conference calls and calendar invites. A little solitude, a little soul-searching, and a healthy dose of "me time", that's the recipe for staying intact in a world designed to pull you apart.

It's not about running away from life. It's about returning, returning to the only space that truly belongs to you: YOURSELF.

Somewhere along the way, I realized -the real promotion in life isn't the one your HR emails you about. It's the one you give yourself, every time you choose peace over panic, kindness over ego, and human connection over cold transactions.

In the world of quarterly targets and perpetual "ASAP" deadlines, your health -both mental and physical -is your only true job security. The emails can wait, the targets will reset, but your mind and body? They're one-time offers. No warranty, no replacement policy.

I used to think success was about the deal you closed or the competition you beat. But life, in its quiet, unhurried way, taught me otherwise. Success is about balance, the invisible scale between ambition and well-being. And the trick isn't grand gestures. It's the small things.

A five-minute call to someone who matters.

A song that lifts your heart on the way to work.

A Sunday morning run that isn't about counting calories, but about clearing your mind.

Because sometimes, the real victories aren't listed on your resume. They're the ones that let you sleep well at night.

And here's my favourite plot twist:

Being kind and compassionate is not just a personality trait.

It's a strategy.

The more kindness you send out, the more life sends it right back, sometimes as a helping hand when you're stuck, sometimes as a smile from a stranger, and sometimes as the strength to survive one more Monday.

So here's what the corporate world taught me, and what I'd pass on to anyone brave enough to have read this far:

Work hard, but don't forget to live harder. Make money, but don't forget to make memories. Chase success, but don't lose sight of yourself.

Because in the end, it's not the business card or the appraisal letter that defines you. It's the people who smile when your name pops up on their phone.

And that, my friend, is the real deal worth closing.

Epilogue
Suit Up, Life's Still Loading!!!

Aman 1.0-free-range childhood edition

I was the kind of kid who believed shoelaces were optional, afternoons were made for chasing shadows, and the laws of gravity were merely polite suggestions. Life was measured in races against the setting sun, scraped elbows were worn like badges of honor, and curiosity was my full-time job. Back then, happiness came bundled with the scent of rain on muddy playgrounds, and the crown jewel of my worldly possessions was my ever-growing G.I. Joe action figure army -a battalion that saw more living room warfare than any General could plan for. It was a simpler world, where the only deadlines that mattered were the ones set by Mummy's voice calling me home.

Aman 2.0-patched, rebooted, and slightly more breakable edition

Life has a funny way of sending you updates -whether you've signed up for them or not. Mine arrived the day a swing knocked the wind, and quite nearly the life, out of me. One abdominal surgery, a souvenir scar, and a crash course in "patience over playgrounds" later, Aman 2.0 was born.

Gone were the days of climbing trees and chasing squirrels; instead, I swapped adventure for observation. If childhood was about outrunning the world, this phase taught me the fine art of outthinking it. Somewhere between hospital beds and homework, I learned that strength wasn't always in muscles -sometimes, it was stitched right into your willpower.

Looking back, Aman 2.0 was less about scraped knees and more about navigating life's version of "Terms and Conditions" -the kind nobody ever reads, until life enforces them. It was my earliest taste of the one corporate truth I'd meet again later: adapt, or be left behind.

Aman 3.0-now with 10% more wisdom, 90% more deadlines, and 100% more wondering where the weekend went

By the time I hit 3.0, I'd been through more upgrades than an iPhone. The shortcut-loving Aman 1.0 had been left in the dust, and Aman 2.0 was still figuring out life's manual. But Aman 3.0? Well, he is a work in progress -always learning, always upgrading, and still wondering, "Where on Earth am I heading?"

The MBA in Birmingham taught me a lot, not just about marketing, finance, or business HR, but about how the corporate world works in its own mysterious, convoluted way. Life there was less about big ideas and more about getting through the next deadline. Convincing customers wasn't so much about passion as it was about convincing them that yes, this Excel spreadsheet really does matter. But you know what? I learned to find humor in it all. Because if you don't laugh at the absurdity of your 3 p.m. Zoom call or the "urgent" email marked HIGH PRIORITY, you'll lose your mind faster than you can say "synergy."

I'll admit, I've gotten better at juggling -and not just juggling tasks, but juggling that delicate balance between "doing my job" and "not losing myself in the process." The corporate treadmill is fast and furious, but hey, I'm on it. Every presentation, every meeting, every coffee-fueled decision is a tiny step forward. And sometimes, that's the secret to survival.

But even as I dive deeper into spreadsheets and sales targets, I'm still holding onto that childlike curiosity I had back in my free-range childhood days. The boy who raced against the setting sun is now racing against the clock. The only difference? The clock is digital, and the race involves convincing clients that your latest report is a masterpiece of strategic thinking. But I'm still here, finding humor in the corporate circus, laughing at the absurdities, and most importantly, keeping the kid in me alive -one deadline at a time.

And from there, the road only got more... corporate.

The funny part? Growing up didn't change the rules as much as it changed the toys. Homework got a new name - "deliverables." Grades became "performance appraisals." Playground skirmishes swapped for boardroom debates.

Even the old game of calling dibs on the swing set evolved into silent wars over swivel chairs.

But the real truth?

Nobody's got it all figured out. Not the one steering the company, not the intern still hunting for the coffee machine.

At the end of the day, we're all just overgrown kids in polished shoes, trying to look serious while life keeps scribbling new questions on the whiteboard.

Some days you ace the test. Some days you just Google the answers and hope for the best.

But here's the real test:

Can you laugh at yourself, dust off, and still show up the next morning?

If yes, you're already ahead of the curve.

So whether you're in your 20s, trading hostel bunks for studio apartments, or in your 40s wondering when Excel became your longest relationship -here's my unsolicited two cents:

Life doesn't come with a user manual, and there's no 'Save Game' button. The best you can do is show up, suit up, and improvise.

And if you ever need a measure of success?

Childhood taught us how to fall.

Corporate life teaches us to fall -and still reply to emails by 6 PM.

The only real assignment, though, is this:

Don't lose the kid in you !!!

About the Author

If you've made it this far, congratulations! I owe you a heartfelt "thank you". Not just for surviving my ramblings, but somehow managing to hold on to your attention span in a world where reels and retweets are the new "book clubs."

Now, a little about me. I'm no author, trust me- I can barely juggle a corporate job and weekends that vanish faster than you can say "deadline." Am I a writer? No idea. Do I have a calling for it? Probably not. Writing a book? Not even on my radar! I didn't plan on this nor did I set out to write a masterpiece. I just started scribbling down notes from my diary -some memories I can recall like it was yesterday, and others, well, they were kindly handed down by my parents (thank you Mummy and Papa). I collected these over time, stared at them for way too long, and voila- suddenly, there's a book in front of me.

Life has a funny way of surprising you, doesn't it? I must confess here that I'm a huge fan of not taking life too seriously. So, if this book can make you smile, laugh, or remember that the kid inside you is still alive and kicking, then I've done my job. Because really, if we stop smiling, what's the point?

So, here's to living with less seriousness and more joy -and maybe a few more cups of coffee!!

– Aman

Reader's Insight

Reader's Insight

Reader's Insight

Reader's Insight